CONGRATULATIONS...
YOU'RE GIFTED!

DISCOVERING YOUR GOD-GIVEN SHAPE TO MAKE A DIFFERENCE IN THE WORLD

DOUG FIELDS & ERIK REES

ZONDERVAN®

ZONDERVAN.com/
AUTHORTRACKER
follow your favorite authors

invert

youth
specialties

Congratulations...You're Gifted!
Copyright 2008 by Doug Fields and Erik Rees

Youth Specialties resources, 300 S. Pierce St., El Cajon, CA 92020 are published by
Zondervan, 5300 Patterson Ave. SE, Grand Rapids, MI 49530.

ISBN 978-0-310-27725-5

Cover design by Mattson Creative
Interior design by David Conn

Printed in the United States of America

TO JIM BURNS

My youth pastor, my teacher, my mentor, my encourager, and my friend. Since 1978 you have been the constant person in my life to say to me, "Congratulations...You're Gifted!" I am forever grateful for the ways you've shaped my life and believed in me. I love you!

DOUG

TO SHAYA, JESSICA, AND JT

As you become all God has shaped you to be, I pray you live daily with an unshakable confidence in Christ and clarity of his purpose for your lives! I love you!

ERIK

CONTENTS

ACKNOWLEDGMENTS

We have worked together for several years at Saddleback Church, and we are grateful for the many men and women there who have teamed with us to make us better men. Many of these ministry partners cheered us on during this writing project and helped us in tangible ways. We are thankful to be part of a church filled with wonderful people who serve and honor God.

In terms of the actual writing, there was one person who was so instrumental he needs to be mentioned all alone. Rob Cunningham went over every single word, helping us craft better sentences and putting much of his life into this book. We're thankful for his skills, help, and friendship, and for the sacrifice he made within his own youth ministry to help with this project. We are also thankful to Allison McCroskey and Jana Sarti for reading and editing and typing and cleaning this book up on their own time. Also, this book will read more clearly because of our editor, Doug Davidson—thanks for your hard work.

It would be impossible to thank all the teenagers who have spent time with us thinking through the material in this book and applying it to their lives. But during this latest round of writing, there were two friends who provided more insight and spiritual depth than we ever expected…thank you to two of our all-time favorites—Delia Baltierra and Lindsey Pierce. Special thanks to Derik and Reggie Hamer, Dylan Maguire, James Stewart, Jason Bohen, Alex Calkins, Trent Frum, Alex Boyd, Brandon Cirbo, Brock and Jordon McNeff, Adam Santos, Garrett Donohoe, Estevan Pena, Cole Johnson, Jackson Carlisle, Nikki Adams, Emily Arnold, Jade Brower, Jessie Forster, Chase and Larson Ishii, Landon Maslyn, Jordon Sharon, Hayden Coplen, Kendall Thrall, Nikki Charest, Bryn Stamos, Amy Belanger, and longtime friend Kelly Perry. And, a special thanks from Doug to the three greatest teenagers the world has known—Torie, Cody, and Cassie Fields.

WELCOME TO AN EXCITING ADVENTURE!

Just by holding this book in your hands, you've set yourself apart from the *average* teenager. Here's why: First of all, a lot of kids your age don't like to read books. Second, those kids who *do* like to read books usually don't choose books that require them to work, think, and possibly change something about themselves. And, finally, most teenagers aren't motivated by the desire to make a difference with their lives. Many are motivated by success or popularity or possessions...but rarely do teenagers desire and pursue significance. This book will help guide you toward a life of significance, a life that matters.

There are amazing people in nearly all walks of life who spend their lives making important contributions to our world. You probably know some people like that, or at least you've heard stories about people who are working to make a difference. One of the common threads uniting all those amazing people is that they decided at some point that they didn't want to waste their lives. Every single one of those people decided they wanted to make a difference in their world.

Does that sound like you? Do you want your life to count? Do you want to make a contribution? Do you want to live in a way that makes this world a better place? If so, please keep reading.

This book is about helping you discover how God has uniquely created you to do something significant. You weren't put on earth to try to copy others. You were created by God as an original masterpiece. There is no one like you—nobody else has the same particular mix of gifts, interests, experiences, and abilities. You are one of a kind, and God is eager to use you—if you are willing to work at discovering your uniqueness. Are you willing?

The book is divided into two main sections. In the first half of the book, we'll consider the many ways in which God has made you unique—what we call your "SHAPE." In the second half you'll focus on how God can use you and your unique shape to make an impact in this world.

But the most important section of the book is right in the middle. That's where you'll create your own personal "SHAPE profile." As you move through the first half of the book, you'll turn to the SHAPE profile pages from time to time and answer questions that will help you uncover the unique way God has gifted you. You'll build on those answers as you read the second half of the book, reflecting on how your particular SHAPE enables you to make a difference for God and for other people.

This has the potential to be a fun journey as you learn, experiment, evaluate, and set your sights on becoming someone God uses. But before you read any further, we want you to know one important thing: You don't have to wait until you're an adult for God to use you to make a difference. That's right, you can be used by God now! God can use your unique personality, abilities, passions, and experiences to help others while you're still a teenager. Don't put it off—the earlier the better!

It's a privilege and an honor for us to walk and talk with you as you learn more about yourself and God's unique plan for you. And while you'll see that there are two authors' names on the cover of this book, the "we" will shift to an "I" throughout the book—and I, Doug, will be the primary voice. Here's why:

Not long ago, Erik wrote a great book for adults called *SHAPE: Finding and Fulfilling Your Unique Purpose in Life.* Erik's book was such a hit with adults that I began teaching it to the teenagers at our church. When Erik saw how I was using the material, he asked me if I would rewrite his book for a teenage audience. Erik could have done it himself— he's actually younger, smarter, and cooler than me (he even used to be a model). But he knew I'd love the chance to translate this material for teenagers since I've been a youth pastor since 1979 and I have three teenagers of my own I wanted to share this with. He was right!

Of course, I didn't have to rewrite every word because Erik was so clear in his original manuscript. I kept lots of Erik's content, and dropped in a few stories of my own that have been helpful when I've used the material with teenagers. So we really wrote this book *together*—and it's impossible to be completely clear where my words end and Erik's begin. If you read carefully, you'll notice that certain sentences seem quite professorial, deep, and thought-provoking, while others seem...well...a bit more like something I would say! But for the sake of smooth reading, we've chosen to write as though you're hearing one voice—without identifying the author of each sentence. There are just a couple of places where we thought it was important for you to know whether it was Doug or Erik writing—so we told you. But most of the time, we didn't.

This one-voice style of writing also helps us protect Erik's reputation. If a certain portion of the book is criticized as being dumb, he can easily claim, "Oh, that part was written by Doug."

We can't wait to help you discover more about who you are and how God can use you.

You really are gifted,
Doug and Erik

P.S. (for teenagers): You'll get even more out of the book by reading it with a friend, so you'll have someone to talk it over with. Or, better yet, read it as a youth group and talk about it in small groups.

P.S. (for adults): If you work with students and want to help them discover their uniqueness by ministering to others, be sure to check out page 187 for a special note for youth workers about how best to use this book.

CHAPTER 1

CONGRATULATIONS! YOU'RE AN ORIGINAL MASTERPIECE

For we are God's handiwork, created in Christ Jesus to do good works, which God prepared in advance for us to do.

Ephesians 2:10

A MASTERPIECE...ME?

During my freshman year of college, I took an art class. I wasn't interested in art at all—but I was very interested in this cute girl who "just happened" to be an art major. Our first class assignment was to go to an art gallery and study different works of art. Even though the cute girl didn't want to go with me (I'll save

that story for when I write a book called *Congratulations!
You're an Idiot*) I made the trip to the fancy art gallery so I
wouldn't fail the class.

Upon arriving I was greeted by the gallery director,
who enthusiastically told me how to get the most from
my experience. I was definitely a fish out of water. I
remember noticing one cool
sculpture made entirely out
of scrap metal, but mostly I
didn't "get it" when it came
to art. I'd look at a painting
and think, "That's nice" or,
"What was he thinking?" or,
"If I swallowed a lot of paint
and then threw up on canvas it would look like that one there." You know, really
insightful art comments.

> I'd look at a painting and think, "That's nice" or, "What was he thinking?" or, "If I swallowed a lot of paint and then threw up on canvas it would look like that one there." You know, real insightful art comments.

The highlight of my visit was meeting a middle-aged
artist named Ray. I was immediately blown away by how
much passion he had for his work. He showed me some of
his paintings with a sense of pride in his ability and confidence in his calling to be an artist. He spoke with conviction that his creations were clearly one-of-a-kind originals.
I was amazed by all he could see in his art, since I could see
only a bunch of different colors and shapes. But like other
artists, Ray viewed each piece of art he made as unique—
not meant to be reproduced. Every time he picked up his
brush, his goal was to create a masterpiece that was totally
original. I learned more in that one afternoon about art
and masterpieces than I'd learned in my previous 19 years
of life. (But apparently I didn't learn enough to get higher
than a C+ in the class.)

A few years earlier, when I was in ninth grade, I had met another artist who changed my life. This other artist was even more passionate about his own creations. His love for me and every one of his creations far outweighed any human artist's love for their work. I'm referring to the God of the universe as the Artist who changed my life.

God and his amazing craftsmanship shaped me into the man I am today and inspired me to want to make a difference with my life. Check out how the Bible describes God's awesome work in the life of a human:

> Thank you for making me so wonderfully complex! Your workmanship is marvelous— and how well I know it. You watched me as I was being formed in utter seclusion, as I was woven together in the dark of the womb. You saw me before I was born. Every day of my life was recorded in your book. Every moment was laid out before a single day had passed. (Psalm 139:14–16, NLT)

These verses make it clear that you and I are special creations of God, the Artist! God didn't create you to take up space or just hang around or become excess baggage on this planet. God created you to spend your life loving him, loving others, and making a difference while you're alive. God began crafting you into his masterpiece while you were still in your mother's womb. Your mom and dad played a part in your creation (I know, sick thought—that's another chapter of another book called, *Congratulations! Your Parents Had Sex—Doesn't That Seem Gross?*), but God himself is the One who breathed life into you.

God is the ultimate Artist, and he doesn't create anything without value. He designed you specifically and originally so you could do something unique with your life, something no one else would do just like you. In fact, God is smiling right now thinking of you as you learn for the first time, or the thousandth time, that you are his original masterpiece. Here it is from the Bible: "For we are God's masterpiece. He has created us anew in Christ Jesus, so that we can do the good things he planned for us long ago" (Ephesians 2:10, NLT).

> God himself is the One who breathed life into you.

Though we may not know each other, I'm assuming you don't want to waste your life. I've never met any teenager who has said, "My goal is to be a loser and do nothing with my life!" Most teenagers have dreams of greatness and want to do something significant. How about you? Have you given it much thought? It's realistic that you may not know what you want to do with the rest of your life, but whatever it is, I'm betting you want it to be good...even great.

If that's true, then I welcome you and invite you to spend some time trying to discover something about your uniqueness. I encourage you to read this book and discover more about the particular way God has shaped you into his masterpiece. Even if you don't like reading, your time with this book may be very helpful to you. Once you discover *who* you are (God's work of art), then you can start figuring our *what* God might have planned for you and the specific way he designed you to make a difference in the world.

ONE OF A KIND

Like the artist who takes scrap metal and turns it into an amazing sculpture, God takes the pieces of your life and shapes them with his own loving hands to be a one-of-a-kind original masterpiece. Congratulations! There is no one else on the planet just like you! Six billion people walking around—and billions before them—and no one is just like you. No one! That's mind-blowing! Think about it for a minute. Try to get your mind around the truth that there never has been and never will be someone *identical* to you. Only *you* can play the role of *you*!

As you continue to read, I'd love for you to imagine we are going to meet at a nearby Starbucks (easy to imagine since there seems to be one on every corner). At this Starbucks you and I order some drinks, grab a couple of comfortable chairs, and pull them by a small, window-side table. I'm drinking a large

"It's a fascinating thing to me that literally everything God makes is unique—every human, animal, flower, tree, even every blade of grass. He didn't clone anything. Even identical twins possess their own individual uniqueness. That ought to tell us that our individuality is a sacred trust—and what we do with it is our gift to God. Our best contribution in life—our 'utmost for his highest'—can only be made as we allow God to finish his work in progress and perfect our uniqueness. To live without discovering our uniqueness is to not really live. I think God is heartbroken when his children miss out on the potential he has placed inside of them."

Tom Paterson, *Living the Life You Were Supposed to Live*

iced tea (iced tea because I hate coffee, and large because I know we'll be together for a while) and you're drinking a _____ (insert your favorite drink). As we hang out together we'll spend time thinking about your life, your uniqueness, and how you can use your life to make a difference and impact others.

"Da Vinci painted one *Mona Lisa*, Beethoven created one *Fifth Symphony*, and God made one version of you. You're it!...You can do something no one else can do in a fashion no one else can do it. You are more than a coincidence of chromosomes and heredity, more than just an assemblage of somebody else's lineage. You are uniquely made.... Can you be anything you want to be? I don't think so. But can you be everything God wants you to be? I do think so. And you do become that by discovering your uniqueness."

Max Lucado, *Cure for the Common Life*

I'm honored to sit with you! I'm so excited to have the privilege of guiding and helping you discover for yourself just how unique, original, and one-of-a-kind you really are. Once you discover more about who you are, you'll most likely do what so many other teenagers before you have done. Do you know what that is? It's pretty awesome—they've used their lives to make a difference in the world. They haven't just taken up space on earth, they didn't just put in their time at school so they could graduate and then start putting in time at some ordinary job. Instead, they've used their unique SHAPE to do something only they could have done, something they were created for. They've put God's masterpiece on display by using their lives to do what God has designed them to do. There are few things that bring me greater joy than helping teenagers discover their unique, God-given SHAPE and then watching as they spend their lives doing what God created for them.

My goal is to help you discover the unique way God has shaped you. If you'll read these pages (while you meet with me at Starbucks) and bring a willingness to learn, I believe you will start finding and fulfilling God's specific purpose for your life.

My new friend, I hope your heart beats with anticipation and excitement knowing that God is going to start revealing your uniqueness to you as the pages ahead unfold.

DISCOVERING YOUR SPECIAL *SHAPE*

As one of God's custom-designed original masterpieces, your potential to make a difference in this world is endless. I want to help you learn that what you choose to *be* and *do* may be revealed by the unique way God has created you. It will become an exciting adventure to take. Over the years many others have taken this journey to...

discover their spiritual gifts,

recognize their abilities,

use their skills,

express their personalities, and

learn from their past experiences...

as they pursued their unique contribution. This search isn't new or unique to the 21st century!

Actually, my hope is that our time together will help you uncover your personal SHAPE. Have you noticed that I've used the word *shape* several times already? I like the word a lot. My friend and pastor came up with an idea that helps people like you and me recognize and remember God's artistic design. He crafted a memorable acronym to help us remember and discover our unique SHAPE. Your unique and personal SHAPE can be better understood by looking at the following five terms and questions.

 ### stands for *Spiritual Gifts*

Question: *What spiritual gifts has God given you?*

If you are a follower of Jesus Christ, you have been filled with God's Spirit. The Bible reveals that God has given you one or more spiritual gifts you can use to build up the body of Christ (other Christians). Together, we'll attempt to help you figure out your unique spiritual gift(s). (That's what chapter 2 is all about.)

 ### stands for *Heart*

Question: *What are you really passionate about?*
The answer to this question would include your special passions or the "loves" of your life. (When you get to chapter 3, we'll spend time talking about what you love to do and how that can influence the impact you make for God.)

stands for **Abilities**

Question: *What are you naturally good at?*
This is your set of talents God gave you when you were born. You're good at something—in fact, you're good at a bunch of things! God doesn't want you to waste your natural abilities; instead, he wants you to use them to make a difference in his world. (You guessed it, chapter 4 is about helping you identify your abilities and then figuring out how they will enhance the unique role God has in mind for you.)

 stands for **Personality**

Question: *How do you usually relate to people and situations?*
This is the special way God wired you to navigate life. There's not a right or wrong personality, there's *your* personality—and it plays a role in determining the way you impact the world for God. (Chapter 5…yep, you're catching on, the chapters go in SHAPE order.)

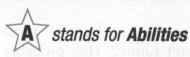 *stands for* **Experiences**

Question: *What have been your positive and negative experiences and what have you learned?*
You have a past—we all do. There are parts of your past (both positive and painful) that God will use in great ways in the future. God doesn't waste our hurts—your past will teach you lessons that will contribute to your future. (Guess which chapter? You got it—all this discovery is in chapter 6. After

my teenage son read this, he said, "Dad, those chapter comments aren't funny." He's probably right, but I left them in to bug him.)

Now, spend 30 seconds and try to commit the SHAPE words to memory. We'll be spending a lot of time looking at these five key words:

S: Spiritual gifts

H: Heart

A: Abilities

P: Personality

E: Experiences

"When God created animals, he gave each of them a specific area of expertise. Some animals run, some hop, some swim, some burrow, and some fly. Each animal has a particular role to play based on the way they were shaped by God. The same is true with humans. Each of us was uniquely designed, or shaped, by God to do certain things."

Rick Warren, *The Purpose-Driven Church*

Before you move to the next chapter, I want you to think about the following words: "I don't have to wait until I'm an adult to figure out my SHAPE." Please understand this! You are a unique, wonderfully complex teenager who has answers to these SHAPE questions now. Your SHAPE isn't fully formed yet—but that's true for adults, too. (I think God continues to refine our shapes throughout our entire lives.) But I want to challenge you to search for answers to the questions in an attempt to figure out how God has shaped you to impact the world in your own unique way.

If you never understand your SHAPE, you may end up doing things that God never intended or designed you to do. When your gifts don't match the role you play in life, you may feel discouraged. (Have you heard the expression, "square peg being pounded in a round hole?") This can be frustrating to you and to those around you. If you don't take the time to discover and understand your unique SHAPE, you may produce limited results with your life and waste enormous talents, time, and energy. I know you don't want that for your life.

As you get ready to discover and maximize your unique God-given SHAPE, I want to take you back once more to the art gallery I visited during college. Imagine for a moment that a portrait of your life (not your face) hangs as an original masterpiece in the gallery. What would you like that portrait of your life to look like? What would be the unique details? What is the title of that masterpiece?

Don't be discouraged if the picture feels a bit confused, cluttered, or blurry. Great art takes time. Don't be discouraged if you're not yet able to see clearly the masterpiece God is creating in and through you. God promises, "He who began a good work in you will carry it on to completion until the day of Christ Jesus" (Philippians 1:6). God will keep working on you until the artwork of your life is more like Jesus himself! (See Ephesians 4:13.) If you're like me, God has a lot of work left to do.

> If you're like me, God has a lot of work left to do.

I hope you will launch into this discovery process with excitement and anticipation, filled with confidence because you know the Master Artist is holding the paint-brush. Think of each of the following chapters as a specific color God will use to bring out the clarity of your master-piece. As your masterpiece takes shape, realize that your personal SHAPE is God's gift to you.

I'm praying you'll enjoy our time together.

FOR REFLECTION, JOURNALING, OR SMALL-GROUP DISCUSSION

At the end of every chapter you will find a special section, designed to help you think a little more about what you learned. If you are going through this material with others in your youth group, school, or small group, this is a good place to share what you're learning with one another.

As we begin this journey, take a few minutes and write God a note in the space below, asking him to help you see how special you are and the specific purpose he has just for you. Be sure to thank him for making you an original masterpiece. (Don't forget to sign your name and date it.)

Dear God,

SHAPE
SPIRITUAL GIFTS

CHAPTER 2

YOU'VE BEEN GIFTED

> "I used to think that God's gifts were on shelves—one above another—and the taller we grow, the easier we can reach them. Now I find that God's gifts are on shelves— and the lower we stoop, the more we get."
>
> **J. C. Ferdinand Pittman**

YOU HAVE BEEN GIFTED FOR GREATNESS

Is Christmas still a magical season for you? If you're like most teenagers I know, you look forward to the celebration, you continue to make a list of what you want for gifts, and you're probably happy with most of the things you find under the Christmas tree. As you've gotten a little older, the holiday has lost some of its surprise and magic since you discovered that Santa Claus doesn't exist (uh...I hope I'm not the first to break the news to you). And you've probably found giving presents can be as rewarding as getting them. But let's be honest, we all enjoy receiving gifts. I'll admit it, I love getting free stuff!

Like you, my teenagers hope for good gifts on Christmas Day, but they don't get up at the crack of dawn anymore to see if Santa has consumed the cookies and milk they set out as a welcome gift. They "get it" when it comes to Christmas and recognize that when the word *Santa* is on a present, it's code for "Bought by Mom and Dad, who are still trying to be cute and sentimental" (or, in our house, "Bought by Mom—and Dad is seeing it for the first time and pretending he had something to do with the shopping.") But even though the "Santa phase" is over, I still smile when I watch our children open the gifts we've given them. As a parent I love the feeling of knowing our gifts have made my children happy. I guess you could say I get as much satisfaction from giving these gifts as my children get from receiving them.

To move on with our discussion of your SHAPE, I want you to do something that might seem a little weird at first. Imagine a huge Christmas tree in the middle of heaven. (Well, I guess you'd have to imagine what heaven looks like first, right?) Picture all of God's children—that would be you and me—running toward the tree to find a wrapped box with our name on it. While everyone is opening and enjoying their gifts, God is sitting by the big heavenly fireplace (no, this isn't in the Bible, but hang with me), and he's smiling and laughing. He's pleased because he knows us so well that he knows exactly what each of us needs. He's not like that weird aunt you don't really know who always gets you new animalroo underwear for Christmas. He's given you a personalized gift that's best for you because he knows you better than anyone, and he knows what's best for you.

This imaginary scene may seem crazy, but in a way, it's kind of close to what God has done with you. When God the Artist began crafting the masterpiece of your life, he made some decisions about how you would be gifted. And the Bible tells us that all people who follow Christ are given unique special gifts (these gifts have come to be known as "spiritual gifts") that help these believers, or followers, fulfill God's plans for them. God didn't buy these gifts at the dollar store, and he didn't "re-gift" something somebody else didn't want. The one who knows you best picked the right gift(s) that would "fit" you perfectly. He placed these gifts inside you when he entered your life and became your Lord and Savior. If you're a Christian and have a personal relationship with God, then congrat-

> The one who knows you best picked the right gift(s) that would "fit" you perfectly.

ulations! You're Gifted! I'm so excited for you to read this chapter and learn more about spiritual gifts...specifically, *your* spiritual gifts.

These spiritual gifts from God arrive with some sense of expectation. It's expected that you would: (1) *Discover* your spiritual gifts, (2) *Develop* your spiritual gifts, and (3) *Direct* these spiritual gifts into use. When you do this, God smiles like the happiest parent on Christmas Day.

One of my biggest joys as a pastor to teenagers has been watching students go through this process of discovery, development, and directing of their spiritual gifts. Over the years I've literally seen thousands of teenagers realize they're not "just" teenagers who are the "future of the church" and have to "wait until they're older" to make a difference for God. There's nothing in the Bible about any age requirement for spiritual gifts. For you as a Christian, the "future of the church" is now—regardless of your age. I love it when teenagers take the time and effort to really attempt to discover their spiritual gifts.

> For you as a Christian, the "future of the church" is now—regardless of your age.

I don't know how much you've learned about spiritual gifts from your parents or your church leaders, but spiritual gifts are important to understand if you're going to discover God's unique SHAPE for you. If you've already learned a lot about spiritual gifts—and if you've already discovered *your* own spiritual gifts—that's awesome! Maybe you can help a few friends learn to unwrap their gifts. But for many teenagers, spiritual gifts are a new and mysterious topic that leaves them unsure how to approach the discovery process.

SPIRITUAL GIFTS—A BIG DEAL

God wants you to understand the big idea behind spiritual gifts because he wants you to put your gifts to use. He doesn't want you to be confused or frustrated. In fact, in 1 Corinthians 12:1, the apostle Paul tells Christians: "Now about the gifts of the Spirit, I do not want you to be uninformed." Like Paul, I also don't want you to be "uninformed," because you'll miss out on some incredible stuff God has planned for your life.

But as we sit together here at Starbucks, I can sense you're still a little confused about this whole idea of spiritual gifts and what they're all about. I totally understand— I'm sure I had that same look when I first began to study spiritual gifts in an attempt to discover mine. Since I've been doing most of the talking, let me take a sip of my iced tea and pause to hear your questions.

WHAT ARE SPIRITUAL GIFTS?

Great question! Let me try to answer by focusing on what they *aren't*. First, a spiritual gift isn't the same as a natural talent. You may be an excellent athlete, musician, artist, speaker, or writer, but those aren't spiritual gifts. (We'll discuss more about natural talents in chapter 4.) Every human being has talents and abilities, but only Christians receive spiritual gifts from God.

> Spiritual gifts work in spiritual ways. They can only be used to their full potential when empowered by the Holy Spirit, who dwells in the life of every believer. In other words, one has to have a personal relationship with Jesus Christ before receiving these spiritual gifts.

Second, spiritual gifts aren't personality traits. Being outgoing and social isn't a spiritual gift. Neither is being quiet and reserved. These are elements of your personality and more pieces to the puzzle of your unique SHAPE (and we'll talk more about that in chapter 5.)

Third, spiritual gifts are different from the fruit of the Spirit described in Galatians 5. Are you familiar with the fruit of the Spirit? It is love, joy, peace, patience, kindness, goodness, faithfulness, gentleness, and self-control. The spiritual fruit listed in Galatians reveals God's presence in your life and this "fruit" can be seen in your character—that's who you are. Spiritual gifts also reveal God's presence in your life, but they are different in that they can be seen in your contribution (what you do) more than in your character (who you are).

So what *are* spiritual gifts? I think the best definition I've ever heard is a pretty simple one: *Spiritual gifts are special skills God gives to individuals to serve others.*

> Spiritual gifts are special skills God gives to individuals to serve others.

Before you go any further, take a minute to reread that definition and then rewrite it in your own words in the space below.

WHY DOES GOD GIVE SPIRITUAL GIFTS?

Another great question! God gives us spiritual gifts so he can use us to help others. In 1 Corinthians 12:7, Paul says, "A spiritual gift is given to each of us as a means of helping the entire church" (NLT). That means your spiritual gifts aren't trophies or medals or ribbons intended to sit on display in your life. Not even close! God didn't provide you with spiritual gifts so you could become popular or successful in the eyes of your friends or culture.

Your spiritual gifts are not for your benefit at all—they are to benefit others. And, you are to manage these gifts so they're used properly and not wasted. The Bible tells us, "God has given gifts to each of you from his great variety of spiritual gifts. Manage them well so that God's generosity can flow through you" (1 Peter 4:10, NLT). You are to use your spiritual gifts in ways that help and bless others.

DOES EVERY CHRISTIAN RECEIVE A SPIRITUAL GIFT?

I love answering this question! Yes! Yes! Yes! If you have a personal relationship with God, you have been given at least one spiritual gift (maybe more). The apostle Paul said, "Each of you has your own gift from God; one has this gift, another has that" (1 Corinthians 7:7). God gives spiritual gifts to every Christian, not just "famous" Christians or "old" Christians or "rich" Christians...but *all* Christians. God says you're gifted, even if you don't feel like you are—so, once again, congratulations!

HOW DO I KNOW IF I'M USING MY SPIRITUAL GIFT(S)?

Now you're asking real practical questions. Nicely done! Here are some ways you may be able to tell if you're using the spiritual gifts God has given you:

1. Other people are helped when you use your gifts.
2. God is honored when you use your gifts (meaning, it's not about you getting credit or glory).
3. You feel good, fulfilled, and used by God when you direct your gifts to serve others.

These three questions can help you begin evaluating whether you're using your gifts or not. But the best way to discover, develop, and direct your spiritual gifts is to get connected with other Christians so they can watch you and experience your gifts in action. Find a youth ministry where you can get involved—one where you'll grow spiritually, where you'll be challenged, and where you can serve. Find a church that will help you minister to others (and express your spiritual gifts), right now, as a teenager! Then, as you seek to serve, you'll be able to tell if others are benefiting from your spiritual gifts. Remember: One of the keys in using your spiritual gifts to serve and help others is to make God the hero.

UNWRAPPING SPIRITUAL GIFTS

Can you imagine letting Christmas pass without opening all those gifts under the tree? That's a pretty insane idea. But that's what many Christians do when it comes to their spiritual gifts. They *understand* the basics of spiritual gifts but they never *experience* the joy of putting their gifts to use. Don't allow that to happen to you. Unwrap your spiritual gift(s) and begin using them or you'll never realize the incredible life the Artist is shaping for you.

When I first heard about spiritual gifts as a teenager I thought I might have the gift of teaching. I didn't know for sure, so I put myself in a position where I had opportunities to teach. Then, after I taught, I reflected on those questions:

(1) Are other people helped when I teach?

(2) Is God honored when I teach? (Is he the hero?)

(3) Do I feel fulfilled and used by God when I teach?

The more I taught, the more these questions seemed to point to a unanimous "yes." But I didn't stop there—I kept looking for situations where I could teach.

> Your spiritual gifts are not for your benefit at all—they are to benefit others.

As a high school student, I began teaching Sunday school to junior high students. It was through that experience I became convinced God had given me the spiritual gift of teaching.

If you want, you can take a spiritual gift "test" to help identify how God may have gifted you. But those tests can't replace the experience of actually serving and ministering to others and trying to figure out firsthand how God has gifted you. Many people say, "Discover your spiritual gift and then you'll know what ministry you're supposed to have." That's fine, but I think there's a better way. I would encourage you to start serving and experimenting with different ministry opportunities, and then you'll be more likely to discover your true spiritual gifts. Until you're actually involved in serving, you're not going to really know how to discover, develop, and direct your spiritual gifts.

As you serve, continue the discovery process by learning what the Bible teaches about spiritual gifts. You need to know what the spiritual gifts are. Study these five Bible passages and make a list of the different types of spiritual gifts God seems to emphasize:

1 We have different gifts, according to the grace given to each of us. If your gift is prophesying, then prophesy in accordance with your faith; if it is serving, then serve; if it is teaching, then teach; if it is to encourage, then give encouragement; if it is giving, then give generously; if it is to lead, do it diligently; if it is to show mercy, do it cheerfully (Romans 12:6–8).

2 To one there is given through the Spirit the message of wisdom, to another a message of knowledge by means of the same Spirit, to another faith by the same Spirit, to another gifts of healing by that one Spirit, to another miraculous powers, to another prophecy, to another distinguishing between spirits, to another speaking in different kinds of tongues, and to still another the interpretation of tongues (1 Corinthians 12:8–10).

3 And in the church God has appointed first of all apostles, second prophets, third teachers, then workers of miracles, also those having gifts of healing, those able to help others, those with gifts of administration, and those speaking in different kinds of tongues (1 Corinthians 12:28, NIV).

4 So Christ himself gave the apostles, the prophets, the evangelists, the pastors and teachers (Ephesians 4:11).

5 Offer hospitality to one another without grumbling. Each of you should use whatever gift you have received to serve others, as faithful stewards of God's grace in its various forms (1 Peter 4:9–10).

From these five passages, you can pull together a list of 20 spiritual gifts that seem to be mentioned. (The list might vary a little depending on the translation you use.)

I've listed them below. Note that they are in alphabetical order—not in order of effectiveness:

Administration	Interpretation
Apostleship	Knowledge
Discernment	Leadership
Encouragement	Mercy
Evangelism	Miracles
Faith	Pastoring
Giving	Prophecy
Healing	Teaching
Helping	Tongues
Hospitality	Wisdom

SHAPE

UNWRAPPING *YOUR* SPIRITUAL GIFTS

To get started in discovering your own spiritual gifts, take a look at the special resource section about spiritual gifts on page 169 (Appendix A). You'll find some additional explanation about each of the gifts listed above that will help you better understand and begin thinking about whether you might have each gift. As you try to discover the spiritual gifts God may have given you, ask God to clearly reveal to you your spiritual gifts and how you might be able to use those gifts for God's glory. When you're done reading through the list and answering "yes," "no," or "maybe"…you'll want to flip over to the "S" page of your personal SHAPE profile, and fill in five gifts you think you might have (see page 101). Then return back here and continue reading.

GET INVOLVED

Keep in mind that answering these initial questions is only the beginning. The answers will suggest some possibilities for what your spiritual gift(s) might be. The questions were written by humans, not God. So, remember that the best way to discover your spiritual gifts is in the context of serving others and seeking guidance and confirmation from the body of Christ (other Christians). Please experiment with these gifts by serving others. When you serve in an area that matches your spiritual gifts, you'll experience fulfillment and fruitfulness (results). But if you find you often end up feeling tired, frustrated, and unfulfilled in your efforts, that may be an indication you are serving outside your giftedness.

SERVE WITH LOVE

The apostle Paul says our gifts should be expressed in love. Whenever he talked about spiritual gifts, he also talked about the importance of love. For example, 1 Corinthians 12 and 14 talk about spiritual gifts, but between these two chapters, Paul offered some pretty important words about love:

> If I speak in human or angelic tongues, but do not have love, I am only a resounding gong or a clanging cymbal. If I have the gift of prophecy and can fathom all mysteries and all knowledge, and if I have a faith that can move mountains, but do not have love, I am nothing. If I give all I possess to the poor and give over my body to the flames, but do not have love, I gain nothing. (1 Corinthians 13:1–3)

Paul tells us we might have the greatest and most valuable spiritual gifts, but these gifts are unusable without love. Anytime you serve, ask yourself, "Who benefits from my actions?" If your actions benefit others, you are serving with love. But if *you* are the person who most benefits from your actions, you need to change something—your serving might have selfish motives. A life of love is the life God uses.

AVOID THE TRAPS

As you start to bless others through the expression of your spiritual gifts, be aware of some common traps God's enemy (Satan) may use to trip you and make you ineffective. I've seen this happen many times in the lives of teenagers who are anxious to be used.

TRAP 1: COMPARISON

This is a tough one for a lot of students. Teenagers who have spiritual gifts that allow them to shine in the spotlight—such as leadership or teaching—might compare themselves to others and develop a prideful attitude. On the other hand, students whose spiritual gifts are less visible (mercy, hospitality, etc.) might find that comparisons lead to a feeling of insignificance. Neither comparison is good, healthy, or biblical. God doesn't create any second-rate art or give out any second-rate gifts. Maybe your spiritual gift is less visible, or maybe it's a gift that often brings attention your way. Either way, don't fall for the trap of believing some people are more important to God because of their gifts.

TRAP 2: PROJECTION

When you expect others to excel in the same areas you do, you're "projecting" your gifts onto others. If you have a gift of administration and you're always organized and focused, that's great. But if you're working with a bunch of musicians (sorry, my guitarist and drummer friends), you might find they'll have some very different spiritual gifts. If you "project" your administration gifts onto them, you'll probably end up feeling frustrated, resentful, or prideful. We are all created differently—don't fall into the trap of expecting everyone to have the same gifts. Be who God made *you* to be, and allow others to be who God created *them* to be. That's God's plan.

TRAP 3: DECEPTION

It's not surprising that one of Satan's traps would involve *deception*. He may manipulate you into believing you have certain gifts that God hasn't given you, which can keep you from growing in the areas where you *are* gifted. Focus on God as you seek to discover the spiritual gifts he's given you and how you can use them for his glory. Find some close friends who can help you stay on track; give them permission to hold you accountable so you can avoid these traps.

As I stated earlier, the best way to avoid these traps is to make God the hero of everything you do and to view yourself as his helper. When we serve with this mindset, life becomes a lot easier.

STRENGTHENING YOUR SPIRITUAL GIFTS

Whatever your gift might be, it's essential to seek out opportunities to practice your gifts and improve your use of them. If you have the gift of teaching, keep learning new teaching techniques. If leadership is part of your unique mix of spiritual giftedness, learn to be the best servant-leader in your youth ministry. If you are strong on hospitality or mercy or encouragement, find new ways to include, care for, and help others in your youth group, church, school, and community.

Begin serving today. Don't wait until you have everything figured out; if you do that, you'll never discover, develop, and direct your spiritual gifts.

God has great plans for your life. He wants to use you in ways most teenagers can't even begin to dream. (I take that back; some of you *can* dream big dreams—but God can dream even bigger ones for you!) Unwrapping your spiritual gifts can become the big first step in finding God's specific role for you.

> "Don't look for God to fill in all the blanks. Don't wait for Him to remove all the uncertainty. Realize He may actually increase the uncertainty and leverage all the odds against you, just so you will know in the end that it wasn't your gifts but His power through your gifts that fulfilled His purpose in your life."
>
> Erwin McManus, *Seizing Your Divine Moment*

The S in your SHAPE is really important to understand, but your spiritual gifts are just one part of the way God has shaped you to do great things for his kingdom. In our next chapter, we'll discuss the things that stir your heart. You'll identify the things you are most passionate about.

One of my passions is hanging out with teenagers like you. It looks like I'm running a little low on iced tea. Let's go get refills on our drinks and talk some more...

FOR REFLECTION, JOURNALING, OR SMALL-GROUP DISCUSSION

What did this chapter teach you about spiritual gifts?

What spiritual gifts do you believe God has given you? If you've not done so already, check out the descriptions of the spiritual gifts on page 169.

Think of two friends who might assist you in discovering your spiritual gifts and invite them to help you consider what your gifts might be.

1.

2.

Identify two actions you can take in the next month to unwrap your spiritual gifts and start using them with others. (Hint: Start by serving those closest to you!)

1.

2.

SHAPE

HEART

CHAPTER 3

YOU'VE GOT A BIG HEART

DISCOVERING YOUR TRUE PASSION

> "The core problem is not that we are too passionate about bad things, but that we are not passionate enough about good things."
> **Larry Crabb**

LET YOUR HEART BEAT FOR GOD

You've probably never heard of Millard Fuller, but his story may sound familiar. Like so many other young people, his biggest desire was to become successful and wealthy. By the time he was 29, he had achieved those goals. But he learned the hard way that being a millionaire couldn't cover up all of life's problems. His health, relationships, and integrity were suffering because he was so obsessed with his career. Realizing his life was headed in the wrong direction, Millard decided to do something about it. So he made some important decisions about his faith and renewed his personal relationship with Jesus Christ.

This new spiritual commitment led Millard and his wife to make other big decisions: They sold all their stuff, gave the money to the poor, and began searching for a way to make a difference with their lives. Eventually they got connected with a Christian community in Georgia, where people attempted to live out the teachings of Jesus in practical ways.

While the Fullers were there, Millard began dreaming about ways he could build homes for low-income families. In 1973, the Fullers moved to a struggling community in Africa to test their idea. Their plan worked, and they were able to build homes for people who could not otherwise afford them. After the success of their project in Africa, they were convinced it could work all over the world. That was the beginning of an organization called Habitat for Humanity International.

Maybe you've heard of Habitat before. Through its efforts, people all over the world (including prominent people like former President Jimmy Carter) have come together to build homes for needy people all over the world. It's been such a success that in 1996, President Bill Clinton awarded Millard Fuller the Presidential Medal of Freedom, the nation's highest civilian honor. Clinton called Habitat for Humanity "the most successful continuous community service project in the history of the United States." That's quite the recognition!

Today, thousands of low-income families have homes because an ordinary guy with a goofy name (Millard) followed Jesus and began to dream about how he could make a difference. Millard said, "I see life as both a gift and a responsibility. My responsibility is to use what God has given me to help his people in need."

During our time together, I want you to think about that same challenge—viewing your life as a gift *and* a responsibility. Your life is a gift from God. But that gift comes with a responsibility to do something with it—a responsibility to make a difference. To do this, there's an important question you need to answer: What passions has God given you? Your answer will be helpful as you discover your SHAPE.

PASSION IS A GOOD THING

God created you to be a passionate person. If you're like any of the teenagers I know (including the ones who run around my house), your life is filled with passionate pursuits. Maybe your passion is sports or music. Perhaps you have a huge passion for video games, or you love to paint or draw or dance. It's not at all surprising that our conversation at Starbucks would naturally drift toward the stuff you're most passionate about. Everyone likes to talk about the parts of life that occupy the largest spaces in their hearts, the things that get them most excited. So what is it that *you* really love to do?

I'll never forget the doctor's visits when my wife was pregnant with each of our three kids. Because of technology, we could see our unborn child moving on a small screen—it was awesome! But the most dramatic sign of life was hearing the heartbeat and watching it pulsate. That

> "Heart is where you are centered, where you desire to serve, the altar upon which you wish to place your talents. Giftedness is what you are. Heart is where you will most likely apply what you are. Heart refers to empathy, attraction, or 'draw' towards a group of people, a field of expertise, or a particular type of service. Evaluating your heart helps you determine where you might best use gifts, where you wish to serve, and whom you wish to serve."
>
> Tom Paterson, *Living the Life You Were Meant to Live*

heartbeat was a simple yet beautiful sign our child was alive.

Did you know that each of us has a unique heartbeat, just as we each have unique thumbprints, eye prints, and voice prints? It's amazing that, out of the billions of people who've ever lived, no one has had a heartbeat exactly like yours.

In the same way God has given you a unique *emotional* "heartbeat" that races when you think about the subjects, activities, or circumstances that most interest you. You care about some things and not about others. That's passion—it reveals the nature of your heart and can provide clues to where you might want to begin serving.

The following three questions may help you discover your own unique emotional heartbeat and passion:

1. What do you really love doing?

2. Whom do you love serving?

3. What cause would you love to help conquer?

Let's take a closer look at each of these questions:

1. WHAT DO YOU REALLY LOVE DOING?

What kinds of things run through your mind when you daydream? I don't mean the daydreams you have in chemistry class every day about the hot girl or the cute guy, or the weird dreams you get after eating a burrito late at night. I'm thinking about those moments when you imagine what you could accomplish in life if there were no boundaries or rules or fears.

If God is driving your life, then many of your daydreams will come back to ideas and thoughts he has placed inside you. Some of those hopes and dreams are right at the surface of your life, and you can easily recognize them because you know them so well and think about them so often. You may need to simply slow down so you can reflect and talk about them. Ask yourself:

- What do I really enjoy doing?
- What thoughts fill my daydreams?
- What motivates me to want to get off the couch?
- Given my answers to the first three questions, how might God use what I love doing to help me serve others?

You might already have a clearer idea of how God can use your passions and gifts to help others. But if it's all still muddy, that's okay; remember, this is a process.

Personally, helping teenagers transform into young adults who own their faith is what makes my heart beat. I live for that! It's a passion that keeps me focused and looking for ways to do that more often. For me to fully recognize that passion, I had to go through the similar discovery process I'm taking you on. I had to hunt for and search out and ask questions to really discover my passions.

It may take time for you to figure out your passion in life, but don't give up. As you begin this journey of seeing how the Artist is shaping you, you may not see the big picture right away. That's okay—don't get discouraged. Pursue your passions, and the ways God will use you will continue to unfold.

2. WHOM DO YOU LOVE SERVING?

Another way you may discover your passions is to consider the places and people you love serving. Maybe you'll find yourself desiring to serve your peers. Think about this—when you walk across your school campus, what do you see? Do you see crowds of teenagers divided into different groups? The jocks and the nerds and the musicians and the loners and the preps and the cheerleaders? Or do you see individual students who want answers to the challenges and pain they face daily? Too many of us go through life casually noticing the external façade of others and miss out on the wonder and uniqueness as well as the hurts and joys each person is experiencing. But when you look below the surface, you begin to see much more than interests and trends. You begin to see individual people and their personal highs and lows. Do you see the hearts of people? Can you see yourself doing something to make a difference in the lives of your peers?

Consider this: Your classmates, your family, your friends, and your neighbors aren't accidental relationships in your life. God has placed these people near you, and he's given you the opportunity to serve them. Seriously! Ask yourself this question: "Who could God be nudging me to serve who is always around?" Think about the different people in your neighborhood or school. Think about that

Your classmates, your family, your friends, and your neighbors aren't accidental relationships in your life.

student who sits alone at lunch every day. You might feel God "tugging" at you to go talk to that classmate or to break from your usual group of friends occasionally to hang out with that loner kid. Or maybe you care about helping other Christian teenagers discover some of the awesome truths in the Bible. Or, you feel comfortable and "light up" around children. Perhaps you want to lead a group of your friends in community service projects. Ask yourself:

- Who has God brought into my life for a specific purpose?
- What peer groups do I feel led to serve?
- How could I serve others in a way that might allow me to use my spiritual gifts?
- Are there other types of people I might enjoy serving? If so, who?

3. WHAT CAUSE WOULD YOU LOVE TO HELP CONQUER?

I know a high school student who has developed a deep passion for confronting the issue of HIV/AIDS around the world. She's made it her personal mission to learn about this worldwide pandemic (the statistics are heartbreaking) and do whatever she can to slow the spread of this disease. Her dream is to see HIV/AIDS wiped off the planet in her generation. She is following her unique heartbeat to make an eternal difference for God. Ending HIV/AIDS has become her cause—the focus of her passion and the cause she wants to conquer.

Remember a while back when we talked about how God created you as a one-of-a-kind original masterpiece? As you take these first few steps and pursue your areas of passion, it's important to keep that in mind. Your path will probably look different from the one a friend might take. That's the way it's supposed to work. You're unique, so your ministry will be unique! Don't feel like you need to follow someone else's passion. God wants to get inside you and get your spiritual heart pumping in a way that reflects your uniqueness. Ask yourself:

- What issue makes my heart beat faster?
- Where could I make the greatest impact for God?
- If time were not a concern, how would I like to serve God?

Here is a short list of some causes that teenagers have committed to championing for God's glory. As you read over the list, if one or more of these jumps out at you, circle them. If the problem or issue that really gets your heart racing isn't listed, write it in the space alongside. This may be the beginning of some further investigation.

Abortion/sanctity of life
Abuse/violence
Adoption
Alcoholism
At-risk children

Compulsive behavior issues
Clean water around the world
Depression/cutting
Disabilities and/or support
Divorce
Drug abuse/recovery
Educational issues
Elder Care
Ethics
Environmental issues
Health and/or fitness
HIV/AIDS
Homelessness
Injustice to women
International debt relief
Law and/or justice system
Loneliness
Mentoring/big brother/big sister
Modern-day slavery
Peacemaking
Policy and/or politics
Poverty/hunger
Racial/ethnic justice
Sexuality and/or gender issues
Spiritual apathy
Violence

HOW YOUR PASSION MAY FIT WITH YOUR FUTURE

When Brandon Ebel was young, he loved music—and everything about it. When his family would visit other people's

> "Our goal here is to recover that adventure God wrote on your heart when he made you. Your deepest desires reveal your deepest calling, the adventure God has for you. You must decide whether or not you'll exchange a life of control born out of fear for a life of risk born out of faith...
>
> So, if you had permission to do what you really want to do, what would you do? Just start making a list of all the things you deeply desire to do with your life, great and small. And remember—*'Don't ask yourself, How?'...How?* is God's department. He is asking you *what?* What is written on your heart? What makes you come alive? If you could do what you've always wanted to do, what would it be?"
>
> John Eldredge, *Wild at Heart Field Manual*

homes, his parents had to remind him not to touch the home theater and audio systems because he was always touching buttons and turning knobs to hear more music.

Brandon's passion for music and technology continued to grow stronger throughout high school and college. After graduation he landed a job at a small record label in Southern California. He had found the perfect place to blend his love for music with his spiritual gift of administration.

Brandon didn't feel "called" to become a pastor at a church, but he did discover God's unique plan for his life. Eventually, he launched his own record label, and today Tooth and Nail Records and BEC Recordings are wildly successful companies with some great Christian musicians—and it's all being done for God's glory.

Brandon didn't sit on the sidelines waiting until he was "old enough" or had enough "experience" to pursue his God-given dreams. He took what he had and gave it to God—and God has used him in amazing ways.

If Brandon would sit down and join us at Starbucks, my guess is that you'd probably listen carefully to him and think, "That's the kind of great adventure I want for my life. I want to take what I love and use it to make a difference for God's kingdom."

You want to live an extraordinary life? Discover your passions and begin the journey to see how they might fit with your spiritual gifts. One day you'll look back on your teenage years and you'll be amazed at what you were able to do for God because you were willing to discover what you love to do and do it for God's glory.

SHAPE

DISCOVERING YOUR HEART'S PASSION

Now take some time to flip to page 102—the "heart" of the Discovering Your Personal SHAPE profile—and answer the questions you'll find there about what gets your heart pumping. Please don't skip this step—filling out the SHAPE profile will really help you discover how the passions God has placed in your heart can be used to serve him. After you've answered those questions, return here and continue reading.

So what's the next piece of this SHAPE puzzle? In chapter 4, you'll see how God can take your unique abilities and add them into this incredible work he's creating in you with your spiritual gifts and your passionate heart. You'll discover how they bring greater color and clarity to the original masterpiece called *you*.

FOR REFLECTION, JOURNALING, OR SMALL-GROUP DISCUSSION

What did you discover about your emotional heartbeat?

Think of two people who have wisdom, support, and encouragement that might affirm what you have discovered about yourself. Invite them to help you further understand the work of the Artist in your life.

1.

2.

Identify two steps you can take in the next week to express your "loves" to help others.

1.

2.

SHAPE

ABILITIES

CHAPTER 4

YOU'VE GOT TALENT

DISCOVERING YOUR NATURAL ABILITIES

"Show me a person who doesn't know his talents or hasn't developed them for service to others, and I will show you a person who has little sense of purpose, meaning, motivation and value."

Tom Paterson

GOD HAS GIVEN YOU INCREDIBLE STRENGTHS

Maybe you've already had "the talk" with your guidance counselor. You probably know the one I'm referring to: "If you could get paid to do any job on this planet, what job would you pick?"

I can just imagine some of the answers the counselor has heard:

- Professional video-game player
- Clothes shopper at the mall
- Mobile-phone tester
- Food taster
- Pillow designer

The question your guidance counselor asks about your future is a really good and important one. The passions we talked about in the last chapter have a lot to do with how we answer the counselor's question. But in addition to your passions, there's another topic that counselor may be trying to explore: What do you do well? What are your abilities? What are your skills? What are your talents? What are you naturally good at?

I have a friend who once told me he took a bunch of tests to determine the future job that would best suit him and the answer came back "underachiever." It was funny and I know he was making it up...but I doubt this describes you either. You're naturally good at something—what is it?

I've met a few underachieving students before, but I've never met anyone who didn't have some kind of talent. I've met teenagers who *thought* they had no talent. I've known teenagers whose parents didn't believe they had any talent. I've observed "friends" who've made fun of a peer's lack of talent in a certain area. I've talked with those who felt inadequate because they weren't as gifted or skilled as a sibling, and teachers seemed to remind them of their shortcomings. But I've *never* met a no-talent teenager.

Every teenager I know is talented at something. Sometimes the talents are obvious to everyone. Sometimes they're hidden. But the talents are there.

You may not have a career or a family or even a car yet, but you're still making an important daily choice: "Will I use my natural abilities (or talents) for God's benefit or for my own benefit?" In fact, you probably make that choice more than once each day without even thinking about it.

I recently came across a statement that caught my attention: "The difference between an ordinary day and an extraordinary day is not so

> "Will I use my natural abilities (or talents) for God's benefit or for my own benefit?"

much what you do, but whom you do it for." That's why it's so important to sit down and think about your talents and natural abilities. The talents you have can point you toward what God may want you to do with your life. They are clues for you! God doesn't waste abilities...actually, he often matches our passions with our abilities.

So you and I are still in Starbucks talking about all this stuff, and I toss out a simple question: "What can you do well?" I'm not asking you to brag—just be honest. What are you confident doing? When do you feel most successful? God has given you the ability to do certain things well. What are those "certain things" in your life?

You've probably already discovered many of the things you love to do, and you'll find even more as you get older. These are often things you look forward to and actually enjoy doing! The people around you know you enjoy these things because you smile, you have fun, you finish what you start, and you don't annoy your parents quite as much while you're doing them. Those are the things God may want you to use in your life for his honor.

That's why it's so important to ask yourself, "Where do I naturally excel?"

Are you someone who rallies your friends to a cause?

Do you enjoy big challenges that need to be conquered?

Does music inspire you?

Are you good at building things?

Are you the person your classmates turn to for help with projects?

Do you view a stranger as a friend you haven't met yet?

Are you always coming up with new ideas to make things better?

Are you good at helping people in need?

Whatever you are naturally good at and love to do is what I want you to think about. Why? Because when you discover it, you can add it to the mix (with spiritual gifts and passions) as you consider how God will use you.

I recently had this discussion with a teenager in our church, and he said all the talk about his talents and skills had him concerned. He asked, "Isn't pride a bad thing for Christians?" It's a good and fair question.

Focusing on your strengths and interests isn't meant to boost your pride by talking about how qualified you are.

Yes. Scripture is full of cautions against the dangers of pride. But focusing on your strengths and interests isn't meant to boost your pride by talking about how qualified you are. In fact, it's really more about God-talk than self-talk. When you talk about your talents, you're singing the praises of the Artist and his design and plans for your life.

I've met lots of adults who didn't ask these questions or find the right answers when they were younger. Now that they're older, it's almost like they've forgotten what they're good at doing. They focus on doing what they're "supposed" to do (yeah, adults feel peer pressure, too) and often ignore the talents and skills God has placed in their lives.

> It's said that nearly 80 percent of Americans go to work on Monday knowing they won't use their skills that week. Don't allow yourself to become part of that statistic! Ask your parents or other adults close to you if they get to use the skills they love in their daily work. If not, ask them, Why?

I have to be honest: Being around those kinds of adults can be a drain. I don't want you to end up like them. I want you to discover the freedom that comes when you pursue the things that match the way God made you. I don't want you to look back on your life or your career or your family with regrets.

EMBRACE THE THINGS YOU LOVE TO DO

Let me tell you about a young woman named Annie. She got involved as a volunteer in our church's youth ministry. She was working with musicians and vocalists on the music team, but it wasn't as fulfilling as she'd hoped it would be. She was a decent singer, but she had more natural abilities as an artist. She liked her role, but she didn't love it.

As she spent time with the kids in our youth ministry, Annie discovered there were a number of teenagers who worshipped God through art. But each of these kids felt like he or she was the only one who worshipped through the display of artistic talents. They felt alone in their worship. Since Annie was also an artist, she realized she could help them. So she took her God-given talent and created an art ministry to help teenagers show their love and awe for God in new and creative ways.

Annie's talents helped others grow closer to God, and at the same time, she was more fulfilled than ever before. She liked her music role, but she loved her art role. She made the switch and everybody won! She used her skills as an artist to honor *the* Artist. I love how she says it: "I could be doing art anywhere, but I have found much more fulfillment and meaning in doing it for God and helping teenagers."

As you think about your own talents and abilities, it's important to consider not just what you *can* do but what it is you *love* to do. Think about that thing that if you had to do it forever, you'd be happy. In just a minute, I'm going to ask you to turn to the back of the book and look at a long list of specialized abilities. It's a list put together by a few friends—it's not the complete list of abilities, but there are about 50 ideas to get you started. God has given out a lot more abilities, but "brains" wasn't one that I got a whole lot of—so I'm sure you can think of other abilities that aren't on the list. God wasn't limited to giving just a few talents; he's given dozens.

Before you flip to that list, I want you to quickly consider the three responses you could give to each item on the list:

LOVE IT! You can't imagine life without these activities. They make your day awesome. Given a choice, you would do these things full-time. (Sorry, sleeping in doesn't count as an ability!) These may be abilities that will someday be part of your career or your big goal in life.

LIKE IT! You may enjoy those, but don't need to do them regularly to feel satisfied. Your attitude toward them is "I can take it or leave it." You might enjoy building things or leading discussions with a group of friends, but it's not something that satisfies you on a deep level in the way the abilities in the "love it" group do.

LIVE WITHOUT IT! These actions leave you feeling tired and disappointed, in comparison with the things you love doing. When you think about these activities, your immediate response is to find a way to avoid doing them. Maybe you can perform these tasks adequately, but you have little or no desire to do them.

SHAPE

LOOKING AT YOUR TALENTS

Now turn to the list of abilities in appendix B on page 183. As you look at each ability, spend a few seconds thinking about whether you love it, like it, or could live without it. Remember: The goal is to discover the things you love to do, not just the things you *can* do. After you've completed that section list your top five abilities on page 103 of the SHAPE profile. Then return to this spot and keep reading.

The way I see it, life's too short to settle for doing things you like or could do without. Why not focus on the ones you love? Imagine a life that is defined by doing what you love to do? God has given you tools to make a difference with your life—so go for it!

Michelangelo (the artist, not the Ninja Turtle) said, "The greater danger for most of us is not that our aim is too high and we miss it, but that it is too low and we reach it." One day, each of us will stand before God and be accountable for how well we've used the unique talents and abilities he's given us. That's pretty scary, isn't it? What will it take for you to live your life waiting for God to say, "Well done"?

Now that you've spent some time thinking about your abilities, the next step in your life is finding some ways to use your abilities to make a difference in your family, at your school, and with your friends. Stop for a moment and look at your list. Do you see any abilities that are a perfect fit for helping your friends? Is there anything that would be great for having an impact at your school?

Are there ways you can use these abilities to help your parents or serve in your church? I guarantee that you can find a way if you give it some significant and serious thought.

Before we move on to the next chapter, let me give you a word of encouragement. You're young enough you may still have a lot of *hidden* abilities. Once you get "old" like me (unfortunately, I'm the same age as your parents—maybe older!), you'll have a pretty clear idea of the abilities you have *and* the abilities you don't have. (Yes, I've had to sacrifice my dreams of being a professional athlete and winning the *American Idol* singing contest.)

How can you find those hidden abilities? Explore. Serve. Minister. Sample. Test the waters. Discover the hidden abilities, develop them, and direct them toward serving others.

And as we'll find out in the next chapter, God's plan for your life isn't limited to your spiritual gifts, your passions, and your natural abilities. He wants to use your personality, too—no matter how normal or how weird—as part of what you do in this world for him. That means God wants you to be yourself and not a cheap imitation of someone else. Remember, you're an original masterpiece!

FOR REFLECTION, JOURNALING, OR SMALL-GROUP DISCUSSION

What have you learned about God and how he wants you to apply your abilities?

Write God a thank-you note for the natural abilities he has given you.

What two people can you connect with this week to review the things you love to do? This feedback can help you determine whether your motives are good or selfish.

1.

2.

Identify two actions you can take in the next week to better express what you're naturally good at.

1.

2.

SHAPE
PERSONALITY

CHAPTER 5

YOU'VE GOT PERSONALITY

DISCOVERING WHO GOD MADE YOU TO BE

> "The art of being yourself at your best is the art of unfolding your personality into the person you want to be...Be gentle with yourself, learn to love yourself, to forgive yourself, for only as we have the right attitude toward ourselves can we have the right attitude toward others."

Wilfred Peterson

EMBRACE THE PERSON GOD MADE YOU TO BE

"I don't have to stand in front of everybody and talk, do I? There's just no way I can do that."

Tyler's a great guy. He loves to help other people, he's always sensitive to his friends' needs, and he has some incredible skills on a computer. But he struggles with feeling inferior because he doesn't enjoy speaking in front of a crowd of people. He gets nervous, forgets what he was supposed to say, and then really feels crummy afterward.

Why would such a talented teenager feel like a disappointment? After I spent some time with him (you guessed it, at Starbucks), it became obvious Tyler got caught in a game of comparison. He watched some friends who were more outgoing, who enjoyed being in front of the crowd, and he compared himself with them. He honestly believed he had to be just like them if he ever wanted to make a difference in the world and even be considered as a student leader and "valuable" to our church's youth ministry.

I tried to help Tyler realize he didn't have to become like them to be valued. I think he was surprised when I told him that everyone I knew liked him just the way he was, and more importantly, God loved him exactly as he was. I think the lights may have come on for him in that moment. But there are lots of other kids who are still in the dark because they believe teenagers are valued for how they look or by the way they act in a crowd or even by what they wear. Those messages may flow from culture or campus, but they aren't found in the Bible. God places high value on the less visible areas of life, and he wants you to be who he created you to be—not some cheap imitation of a celebrity or the most popular kid on the football team.

Just as God gave you unique spiritual gifts, a heart with its own passions, and a mix of abilities no one else can match, your personality is also a unique piece of how God made you. He created your personality and gave it to you to use for his glory. And yes, even if your personality seems a bit weird, you're no accident.

The dictionary defines personality as "the combination of characteristics or qualities that form an individual's distinctive character." These characteristics affect the way you think, the way you feel, and the way you act. Your personality characteristics influence your entire life—how you make decisions, how you respond to new situations, how you handle conflict and resolve problems, how you express your feelings, and how you interact with other people.

Personality "experts" have used creative ways to try to help define unique personality traits. One author characterizes personalities into animal categories such as Beaver, Otter, Retriever, or Lion. Another uses descriptive words like *popular*, *powerful*, *perfect*, and *peaceful* to help define different personality types. There are even personality tests that can help you define and understand your unique personality. Here's what everyone agrees on: Different personalities exist, and when you understand your personality (the pros and cons), you will be more aware of how you interact with others.

> God created your personality and gave it to you to use for his glory.

For our discussion, I'm not really asking you to take some in-depth type of personality test, or walk through the personality zoo, or find some "label" that you should wear to show your uniqueness. But I do want you to learn to appreciate the diversity of personalities—especially the way yours is unique.

Let's face it: We're all different. Walk around your school campus, and you'll find obvious evidence. Some people sit alone, eating their lunch, and reading a book.

> Perhaps you are unaware of the fact that you are the customized expression of a loving God. You have been created with a unique mix of gifts and the desire and drive to use them to make a difference in the world. Your life has meaning built into it. Effectively, you have an exciting, challenging, and achievable future if you will discover and embrace who you were designed to be.

Others always want to be the center of attention with crowds around them. These two extremes and everyone in between reflect the reality of God's design of different personalities.

There is no "right" or "wrong" personality for being used by God. The church needs all kinds of personalities because God values variety. God didn't create other people to please you—and he didn't create you to please them. He made you to please him. When you understand the personality God has given you, you'll do a better job of combining it with your spiritual gifts, heart, and abilities in service for God.

Here are two important questions to think about in our discussion on personality:

1. *How do you typically relate to other people?*

2. *How do you respond to opportunities?*

Let's take a little time to explore about each of these questions.

RELATING TO OTHERS

Do you remember the last time you walked into a room full of complete strangers? How did you react? Did you walk around and meet others with relative ease while asking their names and sharing mobile numbers? Or did you find a place where you could be more to yourself or talk to one or two other folks? Either response is okay. They're just two different ways people might respond to the same situation.

I don't believe in putting labels on people or trying to put anyone into a box that "defines" who they are all the time. But I've worked with teenagers for almost 30 years, and I've noticed there *are* patterns in how teenagers respond to different situations. Let me show you three differences that will help you better figure out your unique personality.

ARE YOU MORE...

OUTGOING OR RESERVED?

Someone who is "outgoing" feels comfortable and actually prefers being around larger groups of people and tends to be energized in those settings. On the other hand, a "reserved" person prefers interacting with just a few people at a time and is satisfied and energized by a deep conversation with one friend. This person gets renewed through quiet, reflective times away from others. Which of these four descriptions best describes you?

I tend to...

1. Find ways to be part of the crowd.
2. Build deep relationships with a few friends, not large numbers of people.
3. Start conversations with people I don't know.
4. Avoid being part of a large group.

If you answered 1 and 3, you may have a more outgoing personality. On the other hand, if 2 and 4 describe you best, then you're probably more reserved than outgoing. God desires to use both types of people—and again, I want you to hear this clearly—one is not better than the other.

SELF-EXPRESSIVE OR SELF-CONTROLLED?

"Self-expressive" people openly share thoughts and opinions with other people—they are able to easily express themselves. People who are more "self-controlled" tend to be less verbal about thoughts and opinions, at least until they get to know other people better. Again, identify your tendencies out of the four statements.

I tend to...

1. Feel free to share my feelings with people I've just met.
2. Withhold my thoughts and feelings from others at certain times.
3. Seek opportunities to share my life with others.
4. Hold back so only a few close friends can truly know me.

If you answered 1 and 3 you may enjoy and find it easy sharing your feelings with others. If 2 and 4 describe you better then you're probably a little more controlled with your feelings. Remember, God wants to use both types.

COOPERATIVE OR COMPETITIVE?

If you avoid conflict in your friendships and try to live peacefully with everyone, then you'd probably fit into the "cooperative" category. You also might accept other people's opinions without a lot of arguing. But if you enjoy overcoming obstacles and confronting new challenges, it's likely you have a more "competitive" personality. You may know kids at school who don't have a competitive bone in their body and others who want to compete with everything. ("I bet you I can get my locker open before you.") What about you? Which of these statements describe you best?

I tend to...

1. Focus on making sure people feel comfortable when I'm around them.

2. Find importance in achievements.

3. Look for ways to make others content.

4. Embrace conflict and enjoy winning.

If you answered 1 and 3 you probably are more cooporative. On the other hand, if 2 and 4 describe you best, you probably have a more competitive personality. Neither group is better than the other...right? God will use both types.

LET'S REVIEW

As you look back over your answers, please understand it's okay if your responses landed all over the place. Every person has a unique combination of different personality tendencies—that's what helps make each of us, well, unique! Your grandma may use cookie cutters, but God doesn't. The questions above were simply to get you thinking about differences you *might* have with others. It's not about finding one label that fits you.

So, based on the answers you gave, how do you relate to other people? As we worked on this book together, Erik and I were aware of our own personality differences. Personally, I (Doug) tend to be more outgoing, self-expressive, and competitive. Erik is more reserved and self-controlled, but also competitive. Actually, he's *very* competitive—he wanted to have a race on who could type faster. What about you?

But personality is not just about how you relate to other people, it's also about how you respond to different opportunities and situations. Let's consider that now.

RESPONDING TO OPPORTUNITIES

The fact that you've read this far into the book is a good clue that you're serious about really wanting to make a difference with your life and learning to be God's original masterpiece. So here's a big question: If you were to picture the ideal way you might serve God, the perfect opportunity for you to make a difference, what would it be? How you respond to opportunities will also reveal something about your personality. These next questions really go to the heart of how you respond to different opportunities.

ARE YOU MORE...

HIGH RISK OR LOW RISK?

I know some teenagers who can't go a day without taking a big risk. (I usually try to avoid these teenagers when they're behind the wheel of a car.) But I know others who tend to excel in situations that are more steady and predictable. In my youth ministry, I've got some students who run toward the high-risk opportunities, while others run away from risk as fast as they can. Which way do you run? Do you enjoy situations that are predictable and where the risks are small? Or are you an adrenaline junky who thrives off high-risk environments? It's not what you want to be, it's who you are.

I tend to...

1. Avoid radical changes.
2. Enjoy chaotic environments.
3. Excel when risk is very low.
4. Get motivated when I have the chance to overcome big obstacles.

If you answered 1 and 3, you probably enjoy opportunities where risk is low. On the other hand, if 2 and 4 describe you best, then you may enjoy risk.

PEOPLE OR PROJECTS?

My friend Josh loves people—all of them. I'm sure he's met a person he didn't like, but I can't find any evidence. He's good with tasks, but he tends to be more energized by working with people instead of projects and processes that lead to projects. What about you? Do you get excited about opportunities that involve lots of direct action with other people or would you rather work behind the scenes on projects designed to make a difference?

I tend to...

1. Embrace opportunities to work with other people directly.

2. Look for ways to complete projects.

3. Enjoy being involved in many projects at once.

4. Find more fulfillment when I can work with someone one-on-one or in a small group.

If you answered 1 and 4, you are probably more fired up around people. However, if 2 and 3 describe you better, it shouldn't be surprising that projects are more fulfilling to you than people. Either way is okay...if that's really you!

FOLLOW OR LEAD?

Did you ever think about the diverse personalities among Jesus' twelve closest disciples? There was Andrew, a behind-the-scenes sort of guy, and his brother, Simon Peter, an up-front kind of guy. Maybe you enjoy following another person's lead (as long as they're leading in the right direction). Or maybe you excel when you're the one leading the group. The only one that is "right" is the one that is really you. Which way did God create you?

I tend to...

1. Often find myself leading others.

2. Feel comfortable when I can follow someone else.

3. Determine the direction for groups I'm part of.

4. Experience fulfillment when I help others succeed.

If you answered 1 and 3 you should enjoy leading. On the other hand, if 2 and 4 better describe you, then you're probably a person who prefers to follow, help, and support others. God uses followers and leaders—as long as both are done with a right heart.

TEAM OR SOLO?

Some people are strongest when working with a team, while others are most effective when working alone. We tend to have a preference. If you feel better doing solo work, that doesn't mean you can't work with a team—it simply means you *prefer* working alone. What's your preference? Where are you strongest? Does being part of a team bring out the best in you? Or do you find you can have a greater impact when you're working on your own?

I tend to...

1. Enjoy being part of a team or group.

2. Look for opportunities that allow me to work by myself.

3. Become energized by being around others.

4. Work most effectively when I'm alone.

If you answered 1 and 3, then make sure you're part of a team when you serve others. On the other hand, if 2 and 4 describe you best, then go after service opportunities that allow you to serve primarily on your own. Either way, God wants to use you.

ROUTINE OR VARIETY?

Some people think *routine* is a bad word, but it really just means you prefer activities with clearly defined expectations—you're not big on being surprised. If that's how God wired you, that's great. And it's also great if you enjoy being involved in a wide variety of projects and responsibilities and activities. So which is it?

I tend to...

1. Be involved in many projects at one time.

2. Prefer completing one project before starting another.

3. Enjoy being responsible for a lot of tasks at the same time.

4. Become overwhelmed with constant change.

If you answered 1 and 3, then variety is part of your personality. However, if 2 and 4 describe you best, then you probably enjoy being part of opportunities that are more routine.

ANOTHER REVIEW

So how do you respond to opportunities? I (Doug) typically prefer opportunities that involve high risk. I love projects, I can lead or follow (if there's a good leader), I like team over solo, and "variety" is my middle name. Erik prefers lower risk opportunities, projects, leading, working by himself or with a small team, and lots of variety.

There is no right personality except the personality you are. What about you? It's not about what you want to be, the right answer is who you really are. What makes a day fulfilling for you?

SHAPE

DISCOVERING YOUR PERSONALITY

Now it's time to flip to page 104—the "personality page" of your personal SHAPE profile. There you'll find the same pairings of personality characteristics we've discussed here. Consider each pair and choose the one that BEST describes your preference. Don't hesitate to reread the descriptions in this chapter if you feel unsure about any of them. Identifying your own personality traits is a key piece in figuring out how you might serve God. When you finish, you know where I'll be waiting—right here.

BE TRUE TO WHO GOD MADE YOU TO BE

God has created you for great works—you don't have to settle for merely "good" ones. In other words, if you're a square peg, don't settle for round holes, and if you're a round peg, keep away from the square holes. If you are more cooperative, don't try to serve in environments that continually require you to be competitive. If you enjoy routine, don't take on things that are constantly changing. I'm not suggesting you can't change or even challenge yourself to develop other areas of your personality. Sure you can! But even if you challenge yourself to be more outgoing (when you're normally more reserved), you'll always feel more "you" in a setting that complements your reserved personality.

The simplest way I can say it is this: *Be yourself.* Don't try to copy someone else's personality. Be the best you. You honor God when you accept your unique personality and use it for his glory. Don't spend your teenage years trying to remold yourself into someone you see on TV, in a magazine, or sitting a few seats away from you in your history class. You'll end up discouraged, disappointed, and defeated. Just be you, the way the Artist created you. Your personality is just as big a part of you as are your spiritual gifts, your heart, and your abilities.

As you continue to explore the creative plan God has for your life, you'll also realize you have a whole bunch of life experiences unique to you. Some of those experiences have been (or will be) fantastic—and some were probably difficult, disappointing, or ugly. Both kinds of experiences are important. As we're about to find out in the next chapter, God wants to use your life experiences as he continues painting his masterpiece in you.

FOR REFLECTION, JOURNALING, OR SMALL-GROUP DISCUSSION

What are a few things you learned about God from this chapter?

How would you summarize your personality?

What types of opportunities might you try out?

Who are two people who could offer wisdom, support, and encouragement to you as you share with them what you've discovered about your personality?

1.

2.

What two actions can you take in the next week that may allow your personality to shine for God's glory?

1.

2.

SHAPE

EXPERIENCES

YOU'VE GOT SOMETHING TO SHARE

CHAPTER 6

REFLECTING ON WHERE YOU HAVE BEEN

"The marvelous richness of human experience would lose something of rewarding joy if there were no limitations to overcome. The hilltop hour would not be so wonderful if there were not dark valleys to traverse."

Helen Keller

THERE IS PURPOSE IN YOUR PAST

If you met Michelle today, you'd never guess how painful her childhood was. Her house seemed like it was always filled with yelling and screaming. Her father was

87

often verbally and physically abusive, and one day when Michelle was a teenager, her dad beat and raped her.

For years, Michelle carried around the pain and wounds of these experiences. Even though it wasn't her fault, she felt a great deal of shame over what had happened. It just wasn't something she wanted to talk about with anyone. But one day, after a friend invited her to church, she experienced God's love and forgiveness and discovered what it means to have a personal relationship with Jesus Christ. In the years that followed, as she experienced more and more of God's healing, she also discovered that the pain of her experiences could actually become a blessing to other people.

Michelle developed a passion for talking with teenage girls who were facing their own difficult home environments. She could sit and talk with an abused girl and share in her tears because she had also shared in the same pain. But she could also share about the God who heals pain. Her tragic past experiences had shaped her for a powerful ministry to others.

I'm so thankful for the important decision Michelle made. She could have become bitter and rejected God because of all the pain she'd experienced. Instead, she ran into his arms and allowed her painful past to become a tool used for God's goodness. Through faith and her experience she came to learn that true comfort is found only in God. And now the comfort she has found is a gift she's sharing with others.

THE ARTIST'S EXHIBIT

In my conversations with teenagers, I often find that one of the biggest challenges can be getting them to take time to reflect on past events in their life. Reflecting on experiences is not something we tend to learn naturally as young kids. Children typically don't sit around and consider the lessons they've learned from what happened the week before. ("I wet my pants last week in kindergarten… hmm…I wonder if that could lead to a life of public embarrassment if I continue in that direction.") But as we grow and mature, it's important to learn from past events.

Getting in the habit of having some reflection time, no matter how uneventful that time may seem, will benefit your life as you continue to develop into the person God wants you to be. You have the capability to review, process, examine, and grow from your past experiences. The learning you receive from a past event can be used by God to help others. And that's true even for experiences that cause us pain. God doesn't waste hurts. The Artist is capable of using events from your life, both the enjoyable times as well as the painful ones, to create his masterpiece: you.

> You have the capability to review, process, examine, and grow from your past experiences. God doesn't waste hurts.

I want you to begin thinking about some of the "defining moments" of your life—in other words, those experiences that have played a part in molding you into the person you are today. Take a few minutes to think about and review them in your mind. What were some of the life events that brought you the biggest joys or sorrows, the greatest awards or losses, the most amazing victories or the most difficult struggles? Reflecting on these will help define who you've become and who you are becoming.

Now I want you to imagine we're going to leave our seats at Starbucks and walk 100 yards to the nearby movie theater. (Go ahead and leave your cup on the table because we'll return to our warm seats shortly.) Today's movie is not an action flick, a tearjerker, or a comedy—though it's got a little bit of all those. In today's film we'll be viewing the defining moments from your life.

You and I pick the best seats in the theater. Before the movie of your life begins, let's discuss what you're about to see. Each of the movie scenes will highlight one key moment from your life. Some scenes will depict events filled with excitement, achievement, love, and fulfillment. Other scenes will reveal experiences that caused pain, frustration, loneliness, and sadness. But every one of those scenes can be used by God to shape you and help you discover how you can make a difference in his world.

As you watch each scene, I want you to think about how that life experience has impacted you. What are the lessons learned from each event? If you don't think you can learn any lessons from your past, I want you to pause right now and ask God to help you learn from your past. The lessons are there—you just need to look for them.

> The lessons are there—you just need to look for them.

This may be an emotional experience for you. But God loves it when you dig below your life surface to seek a greater understanding of all those moments that help tell the story of you.

MOUNTAIN-TOP MOMENTS

The first part of your life movie might be considered a "highlights reel." These are the experiences that brought you lots of satisfaction and joy, regardless of what other people might think of them. If winning the top award for Lego creations at your county fair is a highlight, that's great! God loves you in your uniqueness.

Take a little time and think about your past achievements, experiences, or "defining moments" in these five areas:

1. *Family*: You may have special moments from your childhood or family gatherings that are really meaningful to you.

2. *Friends*: Some of your greatest and most defining experiences have probably happened with close friends.

3. *School*: You don't have to be a straight-A student to have been shaped by events on your school campus or through your school activities.

4. *Extracurricular*: Maybe you've found joy or success in athletic, artistic, volunteer, community, or musical involvement.

5. *Spiritual Life*: Perhaps your highlight was an experience at a summer camp or on a missions trip, or when you found a fresh way to live out your faith and make a difference in the world around you. Or maybe it was the moment you decided to follow Jesus.

In just a minute, I'll ask you to turn to the SHAPE profile pages and write down some of these "mountaintop" experiences. But before you do that, let's watch a few more scenes from your movie...

PAINFUL MOMENTS

This next part of the movie isn't as much fun. I guarantee you, reflecting on your most painful moments can be very difficult. You might even grab some tissues for these particular movie scenes. But if you're serious about discovering your uniqueness and being used by God, you will need to be willing to review the tough moments, too. You need to understand that your painful past events have helped define who you are today.

I'm not talking about little stuff, like that time you stubbed your toe or your balloon popped at the carnival. I'm referring to the experiences that pushed you to your limit—serious stuff like abuse, rejection, betrayal, eating disorders, extreme loneliness, addictions, illness, violence, parents' divorce, death, and car accidents. I'm talking about the hardest times in your life. I've worked with teenagers long enough to know that even a kid who seems happy and trouble-free usually has some deep pain in his or her heart. I'm asking you to get specific with your painful list.

SHAPE

LEARNING FROM YOUR EXPERIENCES

Now that you've thought a little bit about both the "highs" and "lows" of your life, skip to the part of the Discovering Your Personal SHAPE profile focused on experiences. You'll find it on page 105. Take time to write down some of your important experiences, and then use the "film exercise" to really explore a couple of key moments a bit more deeply. After you've done that, return to this chapter and continue reading on page 93.

PUTTING YOUR EXPERIENCES TO WORK FOR GOD

The film of your life is unlike any other. You've got a unique past that influences who you are today. As you continue to think about the experiences from your life, I encourage you to look for how those events might suggest ways you could serve God. You may find that by reflecting on these moments you will see ways in which your spiritual gifts, your heart, your abilities, and your personality have been intimately connected to your defining moments.

Consider my friend, Dominique. For as long as she could remember, Dominique spent every Thanksgiving with friends from her church. Instead of having a huge celebration at someone's house, they got together with many other volunteers to provide a holiday meal for needy people in their community. That specific act of service was a defining moment for Dominique. She said the joy of helping someone and not just focusing on herself is what inspired her to volunteer with a local feeding program once she reached high school.

Like Dominique, Jackson and Nikki found that their experiences shaped their future ministry. When they were dating, they made a choice: They wouldn't have a physically intimate relationship until they got married. It wasn't easy to keep that commitment, but they did it with God's help. Today, they work with teenagers to encourage guys and girls to make the same choice they made a few years ago before they were married.

But it isn't just the triumphs of our life that God puts to use. I have a friend named Nadim whose life was turned upside down when his 18-year-old nephew was killed in a drive-by shooting. Nadim grieved and mourned and cried and questioned and hurt. Then he found a way for God to be honored through his pain. Nadim got a group of friends from his church and reached out to the teenagers involved in gang life through food and a safe place to gather (the church). He helped his church begin a weekly outreach right in the middle of that crime-infested neighborhood. Nadim took his painful experience and allowed God to use it to rescue other teenagers from the same fate his nephew met. He didn't allow his hurt to be wasted.

As I reflect on the painful scenes from the movie of my own life, I can see how my most difficult experiences have shaped my life. I haven't had a lot of pain, but the pain I've experienced has definitely changed me. But my friend and co-author, Erik, has experienced a lot of pain, and I want you to hear a little bit of his story directly from him:

> My parents divorced when I was eight, and my older brother and I had to live with our dad because my mom's salary as a grocery checker wasn't enough to support us. Dad drank excessively every night, then decided to share his inner pain by being physical with my brother and me. Most of the time Dad focused on me—I was the less-than-perfect student.
>
> From verbal bombs that would shake anyone's self-worth to whippings that left welts and bruises, the pain came in a variety of forms. Although the physical marks always healed, the verbal wounds were far deeper, and I've never forgotten them. The emotional intimidation and lack of encouragement finally ended when, at 16, I told Dad I was moving out. For many

years, Dad had told me if I would move out, he would pack my bags. That was one promise he kept—he filled five large plastic garbage bags with my clothes and other personal items and threw them on the porch.

There was a lot of pain in my childhood and teenage years. A friend once asked me, "Don't you wish you had never experienced that pain?" In one sense, I wish I could erase that part of my life. But I also recognize that my pain has made me the person I am today— emotionally stronger and better able to feel the pain of others.

I'm grateful God has now given me opportunities to work with men and women who have been scarred by similar pain. Who better to help them than someone who has journeyed through it before—and survived? Because of my painful childhood, my heart is sensitive to those who have been abused. I can relate to others who have experienced emotional or physical abuse in a way that's possible only because of my own experience. From my pain, God considered it to be beneficial to give me the spiritual gift of encouragement. I use this spiritual gift on a daily basis to help others. I don't believe I would have the unique SHAPE I do today if I hadn't gone through the painful past I did. God has not wasted my hurt—he uses it on a regular basis by allowing me to help others.

So what about you? Can you see any of your painful moments and think of ways God might bring some good out of your hurt? Will you choose to use your painful life experiences in a new way?

You've got a unique past that informs who you are today. As you continue to think about the experiences from your life, I encourage you to look for how those events might suggest ways you could serve God.

MOVING ON

We've spent the first half of this book exploring the SHAPE God has created in you. Together we've considered the unique mix of spiritual gifts, heartfelt passions, abilities, personality, and experiences particular to you and you alone.

Are you ready to take this whole SHAPE idea to the next level? Because it's time to shift the focus to thinking about what you are going to do with all God has given you.

> "Listen to your life. See it for the fathomless mystery it is, in the boredom and pain of it no less than in the excitement and gladness: touch, taste, smell your way to the holy and hidden heart of it because in the last analysis all moments are key moments, and life itself is grace."
>
> Fredrick Buechner,
> *Listening to Your Life*

The God who created you wants you to make a difference with your life. Helping you do that is the goal of the rest of this book.

Unfortunately, if you're serious about not wasting your life, you will run into obstacles and opposition along the way. As we move to the last section of this book and our conversation, we'll look at how to make sure your SHAPE isn't wasted.

There's one last step to completing the Discovering Your Personal SHAPE profile. You'll find directions for that final step on page 109, at the end of the profile. If there are other sections of the profile you've not yet completed, please take the time to finish them before you go on. That'll help you get the most out of the rest of our conversation. When you've completed the profile, you're ready to move on to chapter 7.

FOR REFLECTION, JOURNALING, OR SMALL-GROUP DISCUSSION

What are a few things you found out about God from this chapter?

How have you discovered there could be purpose in your past?

Who is one person who makes you feel safe, where you could share some of the pain from your past? Schedule a meeting with that person in the next week. Ask how you might use your painful past to make a difference in the world.

Identify two steps of action you can take in the next week to use your pain for God's gain.

1.

2.

SHAPE

A SELF-DISCOVERY PROFILE

DISCOVERING YOUR PERSONAL SHAPE: A SELF-DISCOVERY PROFILE

I don't know any teenager who wakes up in the morning and shouts, "Homework! Yes! Bring it on! I love it! I praise the teacher who grants me the privilege of more homework." I understand that probably doesn't describe you, either. But spending some time interacting with what you have read and learned has the potential to be a fun exercise in learning more about yourself, how God has shaped you, and what you might do with your God-given SHAPE to make a difference in the world and to use your life in a way that matters. So don't think of it as homework, think of it as an exploratory adventure.

To get the most out of this process, you'll want to fill out this profile in stages as you read through the first half of this book. Each section of the profile focuses on a portion of your SHAPE discussed in a different chapter. The "S" section focuses on spiritual gifts as discussed in chapter 2, the "H" focuses on your heart's passions (chapter 3), and so on. You'll find the process most rewarding if you read the appropriate chapter before you fill out each section.

SPIRITUAL GIFTS

After you've read chapter 2 and have a better understanding of Spiritual Gifts, it's time to think a bit more about your particular gifts. In the back of the book (page 169) you'll find a section where I've listed some spiritual gifts mentioned in the Scriptures, along with short descriptions to help you think about whether you might have each gift. To start this exercise, please flip to page 169 and take a few minutes to see which items best describe you. Then, when you've finished, list the spiritual gifts you think you may have in the space provided below. (Start with the ones where you answered "yes." Add the "maybes" if space permits.)

1. _____

2. _____

3. _____

4. _____

5. _____

Great! Now dig a little deeper by thinking about how you'd finish this sentence:

I feel I might be able to use these spiritual gifts to serve others in the following ways:

NOW TURN BACK TO PAGE 36 AND KEEP READING.

HEART

After reading chapter 3, spend a few minutes and answer the following questions:

What is it I really love to do? (try to list three)

1.

2.

3.

What people do I most enjoy serving?

What cause do I feel most passionate about?

If I could do anything for God based just on what I love to do, what would it be?

NOW RETURN TO PAGE 53 AND KEEP READING.

ABILITIES

Welcome back! Now that you've spent some time reading chapter 4 and thinking about different abilities, it's time to think in a more focused away about your own talents and strengths. On page 183 you'll find a list of 50 abilities you may have. Take a few minutes to read through the list and see which ones might best describe you. Then, when you've finished, list your top five abilities below. (If you circled more than five of the 50 items, go back and pick the five that most define you. If you've chosen five or fewer, write them here.)

1. _____

2. _____

3. _____

4. _____

5. _____

Here are a couple of ways I can imagine God might use my abilities:

NOW RETURN TO PAGE 64 AND KEEP READING.

PERSONALITY

After you've read through the descriptions in chapter 5, circle the words below that BEST describe the way you relate to others. You can circle the "X" in the middle if your personality style includes both traits. Don't answer the way you want to be, but the way you think you really are. If you need a reminder about any of these terms, turn back to the descriptions in the chapter on pages 73-80.

I tend to relate to others by being:

Outgoing	X	Reserved
Self-expressive	X	Self-controlled
Cooperative	X	Competitive

I tend to respond to opportunities:

High-risk	X	Low-risk
People-oriented	X	Projects-oriented
Allow me to follow	X	Require me to lead
Teamwork	X	Solo
Routine	X	Variety

One thing I've learned about my unique personality is:

I can see God using my unique personality in the following ways:

YOU'VE NEARLY FINISHED YOUR SHAPE PROFILE. I'M REALLY EXCITED THAT YOU ARE TAKING THE TIME TO DISCOVER THE UNIQUE "YOU" THAT GOD CREATED! NOW TURN BACK TO PAGE 81.

EXPERIENCES

After you've read chapter 6, use brief phrases or descriptions to try to identify some significant "defining moments" in each area and write them down. Try to identify at least one positive and one difficult moment in each area—but it's even better if you list more than one.

Family Moments:

       Positive: _____

       Difficult: _____

Friend Moments:

       Positive: _____

       Difficult: _____

School Moments:

       Positive: _____

       Difficult: _____

Extracurricular Moments:

       Positive: _____

       Difficult: _____

Spiritual Life Moments:

Positive: _____

Difficult: _____

Look through this list of positive and difficult experiences and pick the three most significant and defining events. These would be the three that have the most powerful memories and/or learnings. Once you have done this, use the empty "movie frames" on the pages that follow to briefly tell the story of why each event was so significant. Include as much as you can about the experience and the emotions you felt during that time. And try to give each scene a title in the space below the frame—basically, I want you to name that "movie" scene.

• What is one difficult area of life that God has helped you through, where you might be able to help

NOW RETURN TO PAGE 93 AND COMPLETE READING CHAPTER 6.

- What is one positive moment in life where you have experienced so much joy that you might be able to help another person with his/her life?

- What is one difficult area of life God has helped you through where you might be able to help another person?

NOW RETURN TO PAGE 93 AND COMPLETE READING CHAPTER 6.

WRAPPING UP YOUR
SHAPE PROFILE

Congratulations, you've made it to the final step on your SHAPE profile! At this point you've read the five chapters focused on the different aspects of your personal SHAPE, and you've filled in the workbook pages associated with each one.

Now it's time to look over your answers on those pages to see if there's some common thread or clear connection between all of them. I want you to look over your answers and prayerfully consider how God might use your unique SHAPE to make a difference in this world. But I believe this is a bigger project than just your self-discovery. I also want you to share your answers with someone (such as a parent, friend, mentor, or youth pastor) and see if the other person recognizes any patterns. That person may have an inspired idea that might help you better recognize your SHAPE and what you might do with how God has wired you. I've experienced many occasions where teenagers have taken the time to answer these questions but still felt lots of confusion and uncertainty—and it was the help and wisdom of another person brought clarity to the confusion. Don't be afraid to share with a trusted person in your life—they want you to succeed in using your God-given SHAPE.

Final question:

- If you knew you could do ANYTHING for God and you wouldn't fail...what would that be?

CONGRATULATIONS! YOU'VE COMPLETED YOUR SHAPE PROFILE. WAY TO GO! I HOPE YOU ARE ENJOYING THIS PROCESS OF DISCOVERING THE UNIQUE WAY GOD HAS CREATED YOU.

BUT THE JOURNEY ISN'T OVER. NOW IT'S TIME TO MOVE INTO THE SECOND HALF OF THE BOOK, WHERE WE'LL TALK MORE ABOUT HOW YOU CAN USE YOUR UNIQUE SHAPE TO MAKE A DIFFERENCE FOR GOD.

SHAPE

USING *YOUR* SHAPE TO MAKE A DIFFERENCE

YOUR UNIQUE KINGDOM IMPACT

CHAPTER 7

PUTTING YOUR SHAPE TO WORK

> "The more we get what we now call 'ourselves' out of the way and let him take us over, the more truly ourselves we become."
>
> **C. S. Lewis**

MAKING A DIFFERENCE

I hope you're enjoying our conversation. I love to see the look in your eyes as you think about the unique blend of gifts, passions, talents, personality, and experiences that make you who you are. It's awesome to help you discover the particular ways God has created and crafted you.

But there's more. As an original masterpiece, you've been created by God with a specific purpose. Within his artwork is a design for a specific and unique "contribution" only you can make.

What does that mean? Now that you've spent some time discovering your God-given uniqueness, what are you gonna do about it? That's what I'd like to spend the rest of our time talking about.

If you're up for that, let's refill our drinks once more and finish up our conversation.

Your unique service for God, the one only you can perform, is what I refer to as your *Kingdom Impact*. It is the specific mission God has shaped you for. Let's consider these two words: *Kingdom Impact*. When you make an *impact*, your presence is felt—you're making a difference in that area. So, if you're making a *Kingdom Impact*, you are making your presence felt in a way that benefits God's kingdom.

I like to define *Kingdom Impact* as "the specific contribution God designed you to make for him here on earth by expressing your SHAPE." Your Kingdom Impact is the particular way you will display God's love toward others in your generation, through your unique combination of gifts.

I realize that's a mouthful—but there's a lot involved in fully understanding the big meaning of your Kingdom Impact. You might want to go back and reread that last paragraph to make sure you take it in. Then, in the space provided below, redefine *Kingdom Impact* using your own words:

Your Kingdom Impact is way more than what you'll do for a career after college. It is a special prompting from God, based on your unique SHAPE, to make a significant difference on this earth *in a way only you can make.* Here are a few examples of teenagers who got started discovering their Kingdom Impact through some simple, yet world-changing actions...

> Your Kingdom Impact is way more than what you'll do for a career after college.

- Philip collected thousands of shoes for homeless people.

- Jana spent every summer during junior high and high school serving in a poor, developing country.

- Travis organized all his buddies from his football team to care for children in their community who didn't have fathers.

- Sarah raised money to buy blankets and pillows for orphans in Mexico.

- Trevor collected change to assist abused children and give them scholarships for summer camp.

All these teenagers began doing something significant to impact God's kingdom after spending time trying to discover God's unique fingerprint in their lives. They discovered how God shaped them, then put that discovery to use in a way that served others and brought honor to God. They realized they couldn't just "stand on the sidelines" of life when God had shaped them for a game of impact. I think you'll find that to be true about yourself as well.

God is on the lookout for ordinary teenagers (like you and like those above) who are willing to be used to make a difference in this world. From sixth-graders to college seniors, from band members to techies, from home-schoolers to home-run hitters, from students with a C- grade point average to honor students, God excels in using ordinary people in extraordinary ways. That includes *you*! Congratulations!

Will you accept the challenge to carry out your Kingdom Impact? Does that scare you? Excite you? Both? As you think about the idea that God has a special way he wants to use you, take a minute to write down what you feel (interested, bored, excited, afraid, curious, obligated, anxious, etc...).

DON'T LISTEN TO LOSERS

As we begin to talk about your Kingdom Impact, let me start by sharing some good and bad news with you. First, the bad news: There are many losers in this world. There it is—simply stated. Here's the good news: You don't have to allow them to drag you down.

When I refer to a "loser," the picture in my mind probably isn't the same image you're used to seeing when you hear the word *loser*. I'm not talking about the punk kid who sits in your Spanish class and throws spit wads at the teacher, doesn't do his homework, smokes weed, and ridicules everyone who tries to do good. In teenage vernacular, that guy might be a loser. Instead, the losers I'm talking about are normal people in your life who have thoughts and attitudes that can prevent you from living out your Kingdom Impact. For our conversation, I'll define a *loser* as "anyone who tries to keep you from being who God created you to be."

Not allowing those losers to derail your Kingdom Impact will take endurance and determination. While I was writing this book, I ran my first marathon. Actually, I jogged my first marathon—running indicates speed,

> For our conversation, I'll define a loser as anyone who tries to keep you from being who God created you to be.

and I didn't have any (although my time was better than Oprah's). But it takes a lot of hard work just to finish those 26.2 miles. I had to train and prepare and get my body into the physical condition where I wouldn't die before finishing the race.

In the same way, training for your Kingdom Impact and resisting the voices of losers will require the same type of hard work and dedication. Check out how the writer of Hebrews describes spiritual endurance:

> Therefore, since we are surrounded by such a huge crowd of witnesses to the life of faith, let us strip off every weight that slows us down, especially the sin that so easily hinders our progress. And let us run with endurance the race that God has set before us. We do this by keeping our eyes on Jesus, on whom our faith depends from start to finish. Hebrews 12:1–2 (NLT)

To do this, you must throw away anything that distracts or slows you down as you try to run. I've watched a lot of teenagers get excited about discovering their personal SHAPE, and then walk away from their Kingdom Impact because they believed the voices of the losers. Endurance will require that you focus on Jesus' words—not the words of anyone who thinks you're wasting your time or you're trying something too big or you don't have what it takes to do what you feel God calling you to do.

Let me try to get a little more specific about what I'm referring to when I use the word *loser*. A loser can take on several different forms.

LOSER: FOCUSING ON YOUR FEARS

My friend Robert is afraid of heights. He hates them. His legs begin to shake, his stomach turns inside-out, and his heart beats fast (which, come to think about it, is how I felt when I met my wife for the first time when we were in high school). As a kid, he once visited the top of the Empire State Building—but he couldn't find enough courage to get close enough to the windows on the observation level to take pictures of the incredible view of New York City. His dad had to do it for him because of Robert's *acrophobia*.

What about you? Do you have any fears, any phobias? If you're afraid of spiders, you might suffer from *arachnophobia*. Hate to speak in front of crowds? That's called *glossophobia*. Maybe you have a fear of hospitals (*nosocomephobia*) or frogs (*batrachophobia*). And there's my favorite—*arachibutyrophobia*. It's the fear of peanut butter sticking to the roof of your mouth.

Some phobias seem funny because they have bizarre names and seem too outlandish to be true. But chances are good you have a few fears or phobias of your own. (Personally, I'm afraid of walking into a fast-food restaurant and not being able to find my favorite drink, which is called *outtadietpepsiphobia*.)

When we get past the goofiness of the phobia names and move on to discuss our personal fears, the laughter stops. Your own fears are very real and not very funny. I've known teenagers who were afraid to trust others because a parent abandoned them when they were young. I've talked with girls who are afraid to date because they were raped by an uncle. I've known teenagers who never took any risk because they were so afraid of failure. Can you imagine that? Never risking? No risks for God, new opportunities, new friendships, or anywhere else in their lives.

Fear is a big loser.

In fact, fear is one of the biggest losers you'll face in life. Fear confuses you, it knocks you off balance, it makes you forget the way God sees you. And you know what? Fear never comes from God. When you write down all the wonderful, dynamic, imaginative things God created... "fear" isn't on that list.

> When you write down all the wonderful, dynamic, imaginative things God created... "fear" isn't on that list.

I love what the apostle Paul writes to young Timothy: "God has not given us a spirit of fear and timidity, but of power, love, and self-discipline" (2 Timothy 1:7, NLT). As Timothy's spiritual mentor, Paul was encouraging his young friend to remember how God had created him and to not be afraid.

I want to pass that same word of encouragement on to you. God didn't create you to be afraid. He didn't create you to hold back, or to shy away, to run from, or to avoid the big challenges life brings. God never said that those who follow his way won't face tough situations. But God did promise to protect us, guide us, watch us, and lead us through those difficult times.

When fear sneaks up and tries to distort your SHAPE and stand in the way of your Kingdom Impact, I want to challenge you to (1) stop, (2) be quiet, and (3) ask God to fill you with courage and faith. Think about it, courage and faith are opposites of fear—both are saying "no" to fear.

This reminds me of the story of Joshua, who became the leader of Israel after Moses died. Joshua had to fill Moses' shoes (and he was a tough act to follow) and get ready to lead God's people into their Promised Land. Here's what God tells Joshua at that moment in Joshua 1: Be strong and courageous. Don't give in to fear. Don't give in to doubt. Place your trust in me, and I will be there for you. In fact, God tells Joshua *three times* in just four verses—don't be afraid; be strong and courageous.

I wish I could say you'll never experience fear, but that would be a lie. You will face fears in your life, but the Bible gives us clear wisdom on what to do with those fears: "Cast your cares on the Lord and he will sustain you; he will never let the righteous be shaken" (Psalm 55:22). This doesn't just mean to offer your problem to God. Instead, God is telling us to *heave* our problems at him. It's as if God is saying, "Bring it on! I can take your fears. Give them to me. I want them all—throw them at me. They're not going to weigh me down."

> God's enemy doesn't want you to have a Kingdom Impact, so you can expect fear to surface.

Remember: If it's fear, it isn't from God. As you try to discover, develop, and direct your Kingdom Impact, fear will show up. God's enemy doesn't want you to have a Kingdom Impact, so you can expect fear to surface.

LOSER: LISTENING TO YOUR PAST

In the last chapter we discussed how God can use your past experiences to shape who you are. God can use your past to prepare you for your Kingdom Impact. God doesn't waste the hurts in your life. But if you're not careful your past can become an obstacle. And that's especially true when it comes to the mistakes you've made. The poor choices from your past can become losers that limit the Artist's work in your life.

Face it, you're not the only one who has made bad decisions. Everyone makes mistakes. Thankfully, most of our mistakes are minor. But some poor decisions have lasting memories and consequences.

I love the fact that the Bible doesn't ignore or cover up the mistakes God's people made. Here are just a few: King David had an affair and orchestrated the murder of the woman's husband. Moses killed a man before God used him to lead his people. Peter followed Jesus every day—yet he still lost control one night and cut off a guy's ear, then denied he'd ever met Jesus. This is big stuff—I couldn't make up failure stories like this if I tried. I'm guessing you haven't done many of those things I've just listed...at least not lately.

But I'm confident you've made some other choices you regret. You've crossed a physical line in a dating relationship. You've cheated to get ahead in an important class. You've said some harsh words that hurt someone close to you. You've "permanently borrowed" something from a friend (yes, you should probably call that "stealing"). I'm sure you could easily add a few of your own to make this list more personal.

If you focus on all the mistakes you've made, you might decide there's no way you can live out your Kingdom Impact. You look at your list and you begin to feel guilty. Before long you're thinking, "How could God use someone like me? I don't have it together. I've messed up too many times. I'm shaped for nothing good."

Those loser thoughts are rooted in guilt, and guilt is another loser that can ruin your Kingdom Impact. Just like fear, guilt isn't something God created. The Bible says there's no condemnation (guilt) for those who have a personal relationship with God through Jesus Christ. (Check out Romans 8:1.) If you've already received God's forgiveness, you don't have to keep rehashing all your past mistakes. Those are in the past! Meditate on this Scripture for a minute: "Anyone who belongs to Christ has become a new person. The old life is gone; a new life has begun!" (2 Corinthians 5:17, NLT). If you have a relationship with God, you're new...a new person—congratulations!

LOSER: LISTENING TO YOUR LIMITATIONS

When you walk around school, do you ever hear people bragging about their weaknesses? Probably not. Most people enjoy talking about their strengths and try to downplay their weaknesses. I know I do. But there's something good that happens when we give God our weaknesses.

When we operate only out of our strengths, it's easy to ignore or forget about God and rely on our own abilities to get things done. But when we identify and admit our weaknesses and limitations, we're more likely to ask God for help—which is what he wants.

For me, each time I speak to a crowd, whether it's teenagers or adults, I get very nervous. I think I'm going to fail, my stomach aches, and I often get diarrhea (too much info? Sorry). In fact, I hate pretty much everything about speaking until I actually step on stage. That's pretty crazy, isn't it? Part of my SHAPE is to teach about how to be a follower of Jesus Christ and grow spiritually, but I only like half of the experience. There's part of me that thinks, "God, you messed up—why have you allowed me to have teaching/speaking gifts when I'm so nervous and insecure?" But I've learned that when I admit my own weaknesses, God gives me a special type of favor that allows me to continue to live out my Kingdom Impact. While I'm speaking, I really enjoy it (most of the time) and by the time I'm done speaking I'm saying to myself, "I can do this" (that's God's favor). And I think that right up until the next time I prepare to speak again.

You have limitations, too—and they will act as losers in your life if you let them. Instead admit your weakness to God and allow him to be glorified through your weakness. That's exactly what the apostle Paul wrote in 2 Corinthians 12: When we are weak, God is made strong.

Sometimes your limitations and weaknesses are closely linked to your strengths. Maybe you're an incredible musician, but you battle pride. You have talents for writing, but you struggle with self-discipline. You have charisma for leading groups

> Sometimes your limitations and weaknesses are closely linked to your strengths.

of people, but you're uncomfortable talking deeply with a friend.

God wants to use you. You may think you have a limitation that disqualifies you, but if you put that weakness in God's hands, God will use it in a way that blesses others and glorifies him. I know it sounds weird and it definitely flies in the face of human logic, but God wants to use *all* of you—even your weaknesses.

Here's an important reminder: Giving God your weaknesses isn't the same as being someone you weren't created to be. Each of us has natural limitations on our gifts, abilities, and opportunities. Maybe you've dreamed of being a professional basketball player, but you're 5'2". Or perhaps you want to be a pop singer, but your singing scares the neighbor's dog. Or your dreams of becoming a world-famous artist run headfirst into your stick-figure drawings. Let's face it: We *do* have some natural limitations, and understanding what they are is an important part of discovering how God will use us.

But in those areas where God has gifted you, find your strength and pursue how God might use it. And in that process, give your weaknesses over to God, too. Don't try to have a Kingdom Impact on your own power.

LOSER: LISTENING TO THE CRITICS

Maybe you've already learned this life lesson. If not, it will catch up with you one of these days. Here's the lesson: Some people can be really mean. Remember the taunts of the bully you encountered on the playground back in elementary school, or the cutting comments of a "friend" after you tried a trick on your skateboard and fell flat on your face? You still remember those words.

Mean people aren't fun to be around, are they? They spend a lot of time talking about how your idea is dumb, or how your dream will never happen, or how you're not smart enough, cool enough, talented enough, wealthy enough...blah, blah, blah. Here's one thing I've learned during my 25 years as a youth pastor—it doesn't take a lot of intelligence to be critical. Anyone can criticize. But it's much harder to avoid letting the criticism of others keep you from your Kingdom Impact.

Have you ever heard of Nehemiah? He's an Old Testament character who didn't listen to the critics, even when he was attempting to do something "impossible." God gave Nehemiah a huge assignment: Go to Jerusalem and rebuild the ruined city and its walls. That was an audacious assignment.

And Nehemiah wasn't a high-ranking general, a skilled architect, or even a construction-type guy. He was the cupbearer to the king of Persia (the part of the world we now call Iran). God picked a pretty unlikely guy to head up this operation. And the critics knew it.

As soon as Nehemiah began the task, the critics started talking. Some of the nearby rulers mocked the workers, saying the walls they'd build would collapse if a fox walked across them. (I realize this doesn't sound as harsh as a "yo momma" joke, but times were different then.) The critics were brutal. But Nehemiah and his crews pushed forward.

Then a new group joined the chorus of critics. This time the complaints came from "concerned citizens" who said the workers were getting tired. And the whining and complaining got worse and worse. The complainers were losing sight of the big dream and forgetting that God was on their side. They were listening to the losers—in this case, the critics.

The good news in Nehemiah's story is that the walls of Jerusalem were rebuilt, the city was secured, and many people rediscovered what it meant to live their lives in a way that honored God. Why? Because Nehemiah didn't listen to the critics.

If you choose to use your SHAPE to have a Kingdom Impact, you're going to face critics. People will say you shouldn't strive for excellence. Friends will suggest you'll never be as successful as your older brother or sister. Parents may tell you to play it safe and just wait till you grow up. Teachers may say you'll never succeed. Even pastors may fail to see all the potential God has for you.

> Don't listen to the critics, and don't live for the approval they'll never give.

Don't listen to the critics, and don't live for the approval they'll never give. Yes, take wisdom from true friends. Listen to the advice of parents and pastors and teachers. But remember that sometimes God's plan will seem crazy to everyone—including you. Listen for God's inner voice and follow his leading. And that's why it's so important to give God your dreams.

GIVE GOD YOUR DREAMS

One of the top reasons I like working with teenagers is because you still know how to dream. You haven't given up on the possibilities life has for you. Too many adults have lost the ability God gave them to dream about the future.

Children are great dreamers, and I know many teenagers who are, too.

Some dreams seem crazy. I know a guy who wanted to become Darth Vader when he grew up. Seriously! He now jokes about *why* he had that desire as a child, and he still hasn't come up with a good answer.

Other dreams are pretty selfish. If your biggest dream is to get rich and famous so you have all kinds of stuff and end up on the cover of a magazine, you might be doing it for the wrong reasons. I'm guessing "self" is the biggest motive behind those dreams.

It's okay to dream of success and achievement. If you're athletic, it's fine to dream about playing professional sports. If you're outgoing, it's great to dream about being elected student body president. If you write, go ahead and dream about writing a book people will enjoy. If you like traveling, dream about visiting countries around the world and experiencing unique cultures. If you enjoy being outdoors, dream about climbing mountains or creating beautiful gardens or protecting a threatened river. If you care about justice, dream about helping people who have been wrongly accused. If you're passionate about missions, dream of the day you begin working in a country on the other side of the world. If you love praying for

God has put a driving passion in you to do something special. Why wouldn't he? You are created in his image—the only person exactly like you in the universe. No one else can do your dream....If you don't surrender your dream, you will be placing it higher on your priority list than God. Your dream is meant to be about more than itself or you. A God-given dream brings you together with what God wants to do in his world *through you.*

people, dream of the moment when God uses your prayers and faith to bring healing to someone's body.

It's great to imagine where your skills and talents (with God's help) could carry you someday. Success isn't a bad word. Selfishness is.

Here's what matters: Is your dream all about making a name for yourself, or living out the life God's called you to live? In other words, is it about you or God? Remember, God is the Artist who has given you those spiritual gifts, passions, and talents. He's the one who blessed you with your personality, and he's been with you through all of those life experiences. If your success brings honor to him, that's great. So ask God to help you dream big dreams that require the perfect blend of his assistance and your dedication.

FOR REFLECTION, JOURNALING, OR SMALL-GROUP DISCUSSION

What are a few things you have learned about your Kingdom Impact?

Which loser is your biggest obstacle: your fears, your past, your limitations, or the critics?

Use the space below to write God a personal prayer for his strength to overcome these obstacles.

What two people in your life might help keep your soul surrendered to God and help keep you from listening to losers? Contact those two people and let them know about your desire to grow in this area of your life.

1.

2.

YOUR TURN TO SERVE

RESPONDING WITH A GENEROUS HEART

"I see life as both a gift and a responsibility. My responsibility is to use what God has given me to help his people in need."

Millard Fuller, founder of Habitat for Humanity

DISCOVER YOUR KINGDOM IMPACT AS YOU SERVE OTHERS

This wasn't what Jessica had expected. She agreed to spend the day with some friends from church going around their neighborhood and offering to help out with any kind of project people might need done. The church youth group had never done this kind of community service before, but it was Saturday and she didn't have any other plans, so Jessica figured she'd join in.

No one was home at either of the first two houses. The third house had a "No Solicitors" sign by the doorbell, so they decided to pass. At the fourth house, a woman answered the door.

"Hi, we're from the church right around the corner," Matt told the woman, nervously. "We're doing some service projects to help the people who live near us. Is there anything we can do to help you? We don't want any money—we just want to serve."

The woman at the door, Anne, paused for a moment and then said, "Um, yeah, I'm working on some things in the backyard, and I guess I could use some help. Wait, did you say you're doing this for free?"

"Yes, ma'am, we don't want any of your money," Matt said.

"Well, I have a project, but I don't know if you're gonna like it."

"It doesn't matter if we like it, we just want to serve."

Anne led the team around to her backyard, and a couple of the teenagers started to laugh when she pointed to the "project." Along her back fence were eight rabbit cages that looked like they hadn't been cleaned out since the invention of the rabbit cage.

"This is what I was going to work on today. I was just getting started," Anne said.

The students hopped in (no pun intended) and began cleaning. Jessica felt like she was going to be sick from the smell.

About an hour into the project, Jessica's thoughts began to wander. *Why are we doing this? How much longer will this take? Is this the kind of stuff I should be doing on my weekends? Is this what it means to serve others?*

These are great questions. If Jessica and I were sitting together at Starbucks, I might respond by reminding her of a story Jesus once told.

GOD LOVES SERVANTS

> When you serve others, you ultimately win.

If you've spent any time in church, you've most likely heard Jesus' story of the Good Samaritan. Even people who don't attend church are usually familiar with it. That's probably because the story touches an important life principle: When you serve others, you ultimately win.

One day a legal expert was talking to Jesus about the importance of loving God and loving our neighbors (see Luke 10:25-37). This man asked Jesus to help him understand who his neighbor is. Jesus offers the story of the Good Samaritan as his response. The plot of the parable is quite simple:

A man gets mugged while traveling. The thieves take all his stuff and leave him for dead. A priest travels by—but stays on the other side of the road and never stops. Another religious leader comes along—but he also passes by on the other side of the road. Then a third guy walks by (a Samaritan) and stops to help. He offers first aid to the man and transports him to a nearby motel. He pays for everything the man needs out of his own pocket and promises to cover any additional expenses the motel might incur.

Which of those three guys—the priest, the other religious leader, or this Samaritan—was the true neighbor? The correct answer, of course, is the Samaritan. It's significant that Jesus picked a Samaritan as the "hero" of the story because Jews and Samaritans didn't get along too well back then. Jesus' Jewish audience probably expected the Samaritan would be the villain of the story. But the Samaritan was the true neighbor because he didn't make a big deal of their cultural and religious differences—he simply responded to the need. The best way to be a neighbor is to show mercy and compassion through acts of service. For Jesus, serving others was of highest importance.

Most Americans think of *servant* as a negative word. We imagine a maid or a butler or someone who lives in the small house behind the huge mansion. Becoming a servant isn't a career option that makes the top 10 lists for most teenagers.

But in Jesus' story, it's the Samaritan's service that brings the smile from God. This is the pattern Jesus modeled (Jesus came to serve—see Matthew 20) and he established serving as a plan for those who follow him.

It's a natural, human desire to sit back and wait for someone to serve you. We tend to think: If someone else is willing to take out the trash, that's awesome. Go to it, buddy! You want to make breakfast for me and bring it into my bedroom? Go for it—that would also be great! You're going to do my work and allow me to take all the credit? I like you and the way you think!

> For those of us who follow Jesus, serving isn't optional—it's more of a command.

But for those of us who follow Jesus, serving isn't optional—it's more of a command. God wants you to know it's good to be the one working behind the scenes who doesn't need credit. It's okay to do the work your friends think is too insignificant. It's okay to spend a Saturday cleaning out rabbit cages for a neighbor, or mowing the lawn for an elderly couple, or babysitting for that overworked, stressed-out single mom. You might want to underline this: God will reward you when you serve others. It's what Christ-followers are called to do. Jesus set the example by living a life that served others. He told his disciples to serve. And now, in the 21st century, you and I are called to serve, too.

Serving is a big deal for Christians. As you serve others, you'll be given opportunities to show off your SHAPE (in a good way). Serving can also bring you to an "ah-ha" moment where your Kingdom Impact suddenly becomes very clear. You may be serving and think to yourself, "This is it! This is what my SHAPE was made to do! It's so obvious."

SERVE AT HOME

One of the most important places you can serve might also seem like one of the most difficult places. If you're looking for people to serve, your family is a great place to start. Why would God want you to serve them? You might be thinking, "Have you met my little brother?"

Being a servant requires an attitude shift, and I believe a positive attitude is more difficult at home than anywhere else. You don't wear a "mask" around your parents and siblings—they see the "real" you. Our families see us when we're angry and happy and confused and excited. This is what makes it tough to live out a Christ-honoring attitude at home. Family members are pretty good at catching you at your mistakes and remembering them (especially if they're not Christians). There's no question—it's tough to be a Christ-follower at home.

Maybe serving your family isn't so much about taking on particular chores or acts of service (even though those are good things). Maybe it's about following some advice the apostle Paul gave Christians in the early church: "Therefore, as God's chosen people, holy and dearly loved, clothe yourselves with compassion, kindness, humility, gentleness and patience. Bear with each other and forgive one another if any of you has a grievance against someone. Forgive as the Lord forgave you. And over all these virtues put on love, which binds them all together in perfect unity" (Colossians 3:12–14).

That's a pretty cool description of how you might try to behave toward people you love, isn't it? With your family, it will take even more effort to "clothe" yourself with the right attitude. Forgiveness certainly is important in a family, and love is foundational. Serve your family with attitudes (and actions) that honor God, promote love, and create unity among your parents, your siblings, and yourself.

SERVE YOUR FRIENDS

Serving your friends is another big step. Your friends are important. You value the time hanging out, doing things together, and going through all kinds of crazy life experiences. Those experiences are a big part of your teenage years. But *serve* them? Yes! Jesus invites us to always be on the lookout for chances to serve.

Being a true friend means more than just going to the movies or the mall. True friendship is rooted in love for each other. If you are a true friend to others, you care about what happens in their lives—and hopefully they care about your life in return. But even if they don't, true friendship is serving with no strings attached.

You may not consider every kid at your school a "friend," but that's one of the best places to discover, develop, and direct a lifestyle of serving others. Think of all the ways you can help people at your school. These are your peers. This is your generation. You have something to offer and invest in their lives.

Imagine being in the gym, or the cafeteria, or the middle of campus—wherever you'd go to get a "big picture" view of your school. You see the entire student body gathered. They're talking and laughing and joking. Some are at the center of the action, while others are sitting on the edges. (You remember chapter 5 on unique personalities, right?) Look over the crowd. What do you see? What would Jesus see if he were standing next to you looking at that same group of people?

Here's what the Bible says about Jesus' reaction to the people of his own time: "When he saw the crowds, he had compassion on them, because they were harassed and helpless, like sheep without a shepherd" (Matthew 9:36). Wow! Jesus had eyes that saw people's real heart condition. The Good Samaritan saw the injured man with the same kind of eyes. And God has given you "spiritual eyes" to look with compassion on your friends, your classmates, and your peers. Does that describe the way you see the people at your school? Do you see people who should be avoided and ignored? Or do you see them the way Jesus sees them? Do you see others with needs? Do you see teenagers who just want someone to really care about *them*?

Once you see your friends and peers the way Jesus does, how do you respond? Maybe there have been times you *thought* how good it'd be to meet someone else's need, but when you actually faced a real situation, you retreated because of fear or pride. I found a cheesy but simple motto that captures the heart of a servant: "You spot it, you got it." (I wonder if that was written by the same guy who said, "You smelt it, you dealt it.") The Good Samaritan had a "you spot it, you got it" attitude. Jesus told us the Samaritan saw the need (spotted it) and took action ("I got it taken care of"). He didn't wait for someone else to help—he made the first move.

Keep your eyes open for opportunities to serve others with love.

SERVE AT CHURCH

This might seem the obvious place for you to pursue your Kingdom Impact. But I want you to think more deeply about what it means to get connected and serve in your church. Some teenagers think of church as a boring place they have to go each week to make mom and dad happy and insure they'll receive their allowance. I'm convinced church can be much different than that. Church doesn't have to be boring. It can be a place that is attractive and exciting because the presence of God is there in the life of every believer. God isn't boring, so church doesn't have to be boring, either.

But making church *attractive* is different from being *entertained* at church. If you're a follower of Jesus, your purpose isn't to sit back and let other people entertain you every week. Your purpose is to get in the game and live out your Kingdom Impact.

> God isn't boring, so church doesn't have to be boring, either.

A church—and, more specifically, its youth ministry—is a place where you can find encouragement and support as you discover, develop, and direct your Kingdom Impact.

The list of ways to serve at your church is endless. Sign up for a volunteer role where you greet guests. Help with the children's ministry. Show up on Saturdays to pick up trash or mow the church lawn. Offer to pray for other students after your youth service. Assist with a small group or Bible study. Play your instrument on a music team. Wherever there is a need, there is an opportunity for you to serve.

Many, many cups of iced tea ago, you and I began talking about spiritual gifts (chapter 2). God wants you to use those gifts to help other Christians get closer to him. Your local church needs you and the gifts, talents, and ideas you have. In fact, without you, your church and your youth group are incomplete. Something's missing if you don't step up and serve. Find a way to serve.

But don't let your service stop at the boundaries of the church property.

SERVE YOUR CITY

I don't know much about your town. Come to think of it, I probably don't know *anything* about your town. You might live in a small rural community or a big urban metropolis. It doesn't matter. I may not know your city, but I can tell you this: You're surrounded by people in need. Everyone is hurting in some way, and everyone can be served somehow.

Many of the people in need don't walk through the

> Everyone is hurting in some way, and everyone can be served somehow.

doors of the church. They're sitting on the street corners. They're gathered in the restaurants and grocery stores and malls. They're working on their homes or running their businesses or trying to make enough money to put food on the table. Some of these people may come to your church seeking help. But most won't. You have to go to them. You have to pray and ask God to give you opportunities to meet people and serve them.

Reaching your city means going out and finding the people most in need of help and hope, and sharing the love of Christ through caring acts of service.

That's what Jonathan did. He's a high school student who isn't sitting on the sidelines. When he heard about a chance to help homeless people in his area, he quickly said "yes." Now, once a month, he joins a team of people from his church who provide meals to the homeless and needy. It's a way to serve that brings together his passion for helping people, his calm and loving personality, and his ability to walk up to strangers with a smile.

Put your faith into action by serving the people of your community. Volunteer

"He [Jesus] simply taught us the blessed truth that there is nothing so divine and heavenly as being the servant and helper of all. The faithful servant, who recognizes his position, finds real pleasure in supplying the wants of the master or his guests. When we see that humility is something infinitely deeper than sorrow, and accept it as our participation in the life of Jesus, we shall begin to learn that it is our true nobility, and that to prove it in being servants of all is the highest fulfillment of our destiny, as men created in the image of God."

Andrew Murray, *Humility*

with a nonprofit organization. Coach a peewee baseball team. Become a tutor. Join a program like Big Brothers Big Sisters of America. Or simply organize a group of friends and do community service projects for your neighbors, like Jessica and her crew did.

IT'S ALL ABOUT GIVING

God is a giver—it is his nature. John 3:16 is probably the most famous verse in the Bible (although "Jesus wept" might be right up there because it's so easy to remember— see John 11:35). The message of John 3:16 is all about giving. God gave his one and only son, Jesus, because he loves us and wants us to experience forgiveness and an eternity with him. God loves—so he gives.

Life is all about giving, not getting. I really hope you can grasp that idea now, as a teenager, because it could save you a lifetime of disap-

> Life is all about giving, not getting.

pointments. I've known too many adults who didn't learn this principle until later in life (or not at all). They spent years getting and getting and getting, only to realize they'd wasted their lives on things that don't matter. Listen to what Jesus said: "Give away your life; you'll find life given back, but not merely given back—given back with bonus and blessing. Giving, not getting, is the way. Generosity begets generosity" (Luke 6:38, *The Message*).

Don't sit back and wait for tomorrow. This is your chance to discover, develop, and direct your Kingdom Impact. Don't let God's masterpiece sit on a shelf. Don't stay holed up behind the comfortable walls of your church or inside the protection of your home. Give back to your community. Give back to the world around you. God has given you today, and he's ready for you to get in the game—and along the way, he'll help you grow!

SHARPEN YOUR SERVE

Can I confess something to you? Every now and then, on a slow Saturday afternoon, I've been known to sit in front of my TV and watch tennis. Yeah, I realize tennis isn't the most exciting sport to watch on television. The ball goes back and forth, back and forth. The players grunt when they hit the ball, and officials tell the crowd to be quiet before each serve. Truly exciting television. Yawn.

But sometimes the sport captures my attention when I stop to think about the athletes' dedication and commitment. Have you ever played tennis? It's much more difficult than it appears. Hitting the ball at the correct angle, using the right amount of force to clear the net but stay within the boundaries, serving with power and accuracy—these skills require practice, training, hard work, more practice, coaching, victories, losses, still more practice, another dose of training, and probably a little bit more practice. Becoming good at tennis—or any other sport—doesn't happen overnight.

The same is true for you living out your Kingdom Impact. Maybe you'll find serving other people feels "easy" at first. There's a sense of joy and excitement at this new experience. But then one day you realize the emotional high is gone. What do you do? Do you call it quits and find something new and "fun" to occupy your time now that there are no more rabbit cages to clean? Do you sit around and whine about how difficult and unrewarding it is to serve others? Do you complain that you're having a bad hair day? (Hmm, maybe that one seems out of place.)

Or do you dig in deep and stick with it? That's what great athletes do. That's what top-notch musicians do. That's what high-caliber artists and writers and architects and teachers and designers and students and speakers and pastors and volunteers do. They recognize the need to improve. They understand the importance of sharpening their serve.

You and I are each a work of art in progress—God is not finished with us yet. You're a teenager with decades of living and serving ahead of you. It's incredibly important to continue learning as you serve—and that's especially true if you want to be a leader. I like to tell teenagers that if you're going to be a leader, you must become a learner. The moment you stop learning, you will stop being an effective leader.

As you serve others, learn from your victories. Discover where you feel the greatest passion and the deepest sense of fulfillment. See where your investment has the greatest impact. Find the places where your effort makes other people better and stronger.

And learn from your failures. They're going to happen. I promise that you will fail! That's not a bad thing. I can't begin to tell you all the mistakes I've made in my years of ministry. You're in good company! The key is to learn from the mistakes you make. Are you serving in the right place? Is this a square peg/round hole problem? Did you hold on to responsibilities too tightly? Are you serving in this area for the wrong reason? God knows you'll make mistakes, and he still loves you. Your shortcomings can become a tool you use to sharpen your serve.

God designed us to serve one another—and you can't do that well if you're flying solo all the time. No matter

> God designed us to serve one another—and you can't do that well if you're flying solo all the time.

what you've heard, you're not meant to be a "Lone Ranger" Christian. Sharpening your serve and improving your Kingdom Impact seems to happen best when you're connected with others. A good team will make you stronger, and you can help strengthen your teammates. In the next chapter, we'll talk about how to build a support system—a caring community—around you. With the right team on your side, you'll be amazed at what God can do in and through you.

FOR REFLECTION, JOURNALING, OR SMALL-GROUP DISCUSSION

What are a few things you have learned about God from this chapter?

How can you find a way to serve someone this week?

Think of two people in your life who model servanthood. Ask them how they keep their hearts motivated to serve. Note any new insights you receive.

1.

2.

What are two steps of faith you can take to serve your family, your friends, your church, or your community?

1.

2.

YOU'RE BETTER TOGETHER

STRONG FRIENDSHIPS INSPIRE YOUR SHAPE

Friends come and friends go,
but a true friend sticks by you
like family.

Proverbs 18:24,
The Message

YOU NEED A TEAM

Chuck was injured. He hadn't been able to walk for several years. Doctors said he was paralyzed and there was nothing they could do. Not surprisingly, Chuck wasn't happy with the doctors' news. He wanted to walk again, more than anything he could imagine.

One day, several friends stopped by to see how Chuck was doing. It wasn't

147

one of his good days—Chuck seemed depressed and pessimistic. "It's hopeless," he kept saying. "My life is never going to change."

Thankfully, his friends were a bit more optimistic. They wanted to see Chuck walk again, too, and they hated to see him so discouraged. Jose said he'd seen a report on TV about a preacher-guy who might be able to help. Apparently, this man was responsible for all types of healings. It sounded wild, but maybe they should take a risk and get Chuck to see this miracle worker. What did they have to lose?

They checked out the healer's Web site and were excited to see he was preaching nearby that afternoon. Although it was a crazy idea, all the guys agreed they would do the possible and get Chuck there, to see if this preacher/healer could do the impossible.

They moved Chuck to a cot and each of the four guys grabbed a corner and headed outside. When they arrived at the healer's location, they were surprised how big the crowd was. It was standing room only, with people flowing outside. There was no way they would ever make it through the doors to see the preacher/healer—they were already jammed full of other hurting people. They felt stuck, and the little glimmer of hope Chuck had felt when they began the unlikely trip was fading fast.

Suddenly, Jose had a wild idea—even wilder than what they were already doing. Jose had noticed a fire escape on the back side of the building. He thought, "What if we climb up and try to find a way to get Chuck into the room from the *top* of the building?"

Although it sounded insane, the other friends agreed. "Let's give it a try. We're already here—why not go for it?"

As they carefully maneuvered their way up the fire escape stairs carrying Chuck on the bed, all the guys were laughing and sweating. Jacob said, "Well, the good news is if we drop Chuck, he won't feel a thing." Everyone laughed again, although Chuck was doing more praying than laughing. He understood that the situation was pretty odd, but he desperately wanted their plan to work.

When the friends got to the roof of the building, they realized there was no easy, clear-cut access inside. So, in desperation, they began to tear the roof tiles to create a new skylight. Tile after tile came off, until finally they'd created a hole big enough to let them do the unthinkable: They found some rope and lowered Chuck into the room.

Can you picture it? In the middle of a packed house, Chuck was lowered through the ceiling until he came face to face with the preacher-man. His name was Jesus.

Jesus told Chuck his sins were forgiven. Then he told Chuck to stand up and walk. To everyone's surprise the impossible happened. Chuck walked. He was healed. He even began jumping up and down and praising God for his miraculous healing. It was a great display of friendship and the power of the God-man, Jesus.

Granted, I've changed a couple of details in my retelling of this event that happened over 2,000 years ago. For the original story, you can check out Luke chapter 5—and don't be surprised if you don't see the name "Chuck." I changed some specifics in the story for you, but the Bible makes it very clear the paralyzed man wouldn't have experienced Jesus' healing without the help of some risk-taking friends. The man needed Jesus' healing (the impossible), but he also needed a team to get him to Jesus (the possible). He was a healed person because his friends cared enough to work together for his benefit.

What about your life? Where do you turn when you need help? Is there a friend, a coach, or a pastor? Maybe you have a teacher, a neighbor, or someone in your small group? Bottom line, you need people in your life who will support you as you begin to express your SHAPE.

Wanting to have a close friend or group of friends isn't selfish. Healthy relationships with other people are a basic necessity if you're alive and breathing. Everyone needs good friends. We need people who believe in us, who enjoy being around us, who are willing to help us, laugh with us, and loan us their video games. Life just wouldn't be as rich and rewarding without friends.

> You need people in your life who will support you as you begin to express your SHAPE.

Good friends will not only inspire you to discover your unique SHAPE, but will also help and challenge you to live it out for your Kingdom Impact. Everyone needs someone else to go through life with them! Why? Because you're better together!

GOOD FRIENDS CAN HELP YOUR KINGDOM IMPACT

Life is much more fun when you're part of a team. I grew up playing sports so I use a lot of sports metaphors when I speak and write. Imagine playing baseball by yourself. Solo dodgeball gets boring fast (and tiring when you have to chase the ball you threw at no one). It's tough to play both sides of the volleyball net, right? Pitchers need catchers. Forwards need guards. Linemen need quarterbacks. Setters need outside hitters. Defensemen need goalies.

Even athletes in seemingly "individual" sports (such as tennis, golf, or running) require others if they're going to be successful. The world's best golfers, runners, and tennis players all have coaches, trainers, and managers. And every athlete will tell you how much it helps to have fans or cheerleaders encouraging them and spurring them on. One person may "compete," but the entire team is part of the process.

You were designed to be part of a team. God wants to surround you with people who will be part of your life—people who can help you discover your SHAPE and live out your Kingdom Impact. The Bible says, "And let us consider how we may spur one another on toward love and good deeds, not giving up meeting together, as some are in the habit of doing, but encouraging one another—and all the more as you see the Day approaching" (Hebrews 10:24–25).

Your team might be a few close friends you can rely on. It might be your small group from church. It could be a group of students who volunteer at a soup kitchen or a bunch of student leaders who make your school a better place. It might be a ministry team at your church. This team is simply a group of people committed to a common cause and to one another. Think about this verse from the Bible: "By yourself you're unprotected. With a friend you can face the worst. Can you round up a third? A three-stranded rope isn't easily snapped" (Ecclesiastes 4:12, *The Message*). That's a great image of friendship.

On any given day, your team of friends can provide great inspiration to you. In an emergency, your team becomes a form of spiritual life support, helping you survive. A healthy friendship team is a place where the "three-stranded rope" is put to the test—and passes. Good friendships help you so you don't snap. In order for you to live out your unique God-given SHAPE, you need a team of friends who become better when they come together. And, you need to play your part on the team.

PLAY YOUR PART ON THE TEAM

The New Testament is filled with the apostle Paul's writings. Paul was a genius at using analogies to help us understand biblical truth. One of Paul's most well-known ones is found in 1 Corinthians 12, where he compares the body of Christ—everyone who's a Christian—with the human body. He notes that each human body part has an important role to play, regardless of its visibility. The body doesn't just need the eye, the nose, or the hand. All the body parts are needed! If the body were just one big foot, it wouldn't be effective (and it would be quite gross).

Paul says the same is true in the body of Christ. Each of us has a unique role to play. That's another reason it's important to discover your particular SHAPE. You have a part to play in the body!

But how about this thought: If some people are ears or eyes, and others are feet or hands, who is the pinky toe? Who gets to be the left kidney? Is there a "spiritual" pancreas or leg bone or knee or even the colon?

OK, I'll admit I might be thinking about this a little too hard. But hang with me for a moment. It's not tough being a hand or eye or foot. Those body parts are used often, and we're pretty aware of them. But what about the less visible body parts, the ones that get very little attention? You probably don't spend much time thinking about your kidney or leg bone or little toe...unless there's a problem! If that body part stops working well, you are suddenly very aware of it!

When your body functions properly, doctors call that "health." That's what you're looking for in a friendship. You want friendships where everyone (including you) plays a part and no one thinks he or she is "the only one" that's important. Healthy friendships support one another.

In football, people pay a lot of attention to the quarterback. He's the guiding force on the field and executes the plays. But the quarterback needs wide receivers and running backs to help score touchdowns. He needs blockers to keep him from getting tackled immediately, every time he touches the ball. And he also needs linebackers and defensive tackles to stop the other team from scoring. No football team can win with just a quarterback, and your team can't win unless everyone plays his or her position—even if it's not the "star" role on the team. A healthy team recognizes the value each person brings. Play your part, and your friendship team will be stronger.

> A healthy team recognizes the value each person brings. Play your part, and your friendship team will be stronger.

STRENGTHEN YOUR TEAM

You have something important to offer. Your team needs you. That's really the message I've been trying to get you to embrace during our whole Starbucks conversation. God formed you with a unique combination of spiritual gifts, passions, abilities, personality traits, and experiences. His creative plan is for you to take your life and invest it in others by serving them and helping each of them discover, develop, and direct his or her *own* Kingdom Impact. Those people then do the same with others, and the process repeats over and over and over.

Pray for God's blessing on your friendships. Pray for your friends, asking God to help them experience stronger and deeper relationships with him and with the people around them. Spend time with God each day asking him to protect, guide, and direct them.

Look for ways to invest your time in friends' lives. Years from now, you may forget what you learned in English or math or history (if you haven't already), but you'll never forget the late-night conversations, the crazy moments, the incredible experiences that left you with a sense of belonging and connectedness with a friend. Just being there for one another is a huge investment you can make.

Discovering, developing, and directing your own Kingdom Impact is another important way to invest in the lives of your friends. Have you ever noticed that when you spend time around people who are growing spiritually, you want to grow, too? Train with a better athlete, and you'll get stronger. Perform with a better musician, and your skills will improve. Observe a better painter, and you'll learn new ways to communicate through art. Keep growing. Continue to sharpen your serve and it will become an investment that will benefit you *and* your friends.

Our conversation is nearing its end, but I want to leave you with just a few words of wisdom and encouragement to take with you (that means there's only one more chapter). I don't want you to walk away from our long conversation and do nothing. I want you to put these ideas into practice. Who knows? Maybe you'll change your world!

FOR REFLECTION, JOURNALING, OR SMALL-GROUP DISCUSSION

What are a few things you learned from this chapter about the importance of having good friendships?

Write a thank-you note to God for one person who recently has helped you in a time of need. Then write a thank-you note to that person.

Think of two people you know who inspire in the way they care about their friends and others close to them. What do you think it is about them that makes a difference?

1.

2.

How can you make an investment in someone else this week?

Spend some time asking God for the wisdom and strength you need to develop healthy friendships.

CHAPTER 10

CHANGE YOUR WORLD

LET YOUR KINGDOM IMPACT BEGIN NOW!

"...being confident of this, that he who began a good work in you will carry it on to completion until the day of Christ Jesus."

Philippians 1:6

GOD IS READY FOR YOU TO SERVE TODAY

I don't remember much from that art class I took in college. (Remember my experience in chapter 1?) But there is one image from that art class I can still see clearly in my mind today: I remember noticing there were several unfinished pottery pieces scattered around the classroom. Something obviously had gone wrong somewhere during those projects that caused students to abandon their creations. The partially shaped pots had collapsed, the clay hardened, and they were left as worthless lumps. It was a sad sight. Attempts at art—alone, broken, with no one caring enough to claim them.

Have you ever felt really alone? Have you ever felt unwanted? Perhaps you literally were abandoned as a child by your mom or dad. Or, maybe along the way, you had some "friends" who showed they really weren't friends by being less than faithful and excluding you from their group. Everyone I know has experienced some moments of loneliness. Sometimes it can even feel like God is nowhere to be found.

The great news I want you to remember is God doesn't leave his masterpieces alone or unfinished. Let's take another look at the verse from Philippians that's quoted at the very beginning of this chapter. I love the way it's worded in *The Message*: "There has never been the slightest doubt in my mind that the God who started this great work in you would keep at it and bring it to a flourishing finish on the very day Christ Jesus appears" (Philippians 1:6, *The Message*). When God starts a project (such as *you*), he doesn't abandon it. His plans are to bring it to completion. There is no doubt about it.

> God's plan for your life is long-term and big-picture.

God's plan for your life is long-term and big-picture. He is the Artist who began this project called "you," and he's the Artist who will see it through until completion. At times, you may think his plans have changed or that he's decided his earlier idea was a mistake. But you can be confident God knows what he's doing.

There have been many moments in my life when I wondered what God was doing. I'd pray for a door to open—but it wouldn't open. I'd be convinced of my next step for a project—and things would suddenly change. I'd be thinking, "God, what are you doing? Why aren't you orchestrating my life like I think it should go?" Fortunately, since I've been a follower of Jesus since ninth grade, those times when I couldn't see what God had in mind for me have helped provide me a greater understanding of Proverbs 16:9: "We can make our plans, but the Lord determines our steps" (NLT).

If you are going to reach your full potential as a follower of Jesus who discovers, develops, and directs his or her SHAPE, you will need to stay on the potter's wheel. Artists who work with clay use a potter's wheel to turn the clay as they mold it. While the clay is on the wheel, the artist can continue creating. Once the clay is off the wheel, it will harden and no longer be moldable. What I'm suggesting is for you to stay connected to God and stay close to him so you remain moldable in his hands. That's where God wants you to be as he continues his work of completing your SHAPE for your Kingdom Impact.

ONE IS A BIG NUMBER

As you and I sit in Starbucks, nearing the end of our time together, you ask me a question I've heard many times from other teenagers: "I get the idea of SHAPE, but how can God use me for a Kingdom Impact when I'm just one person?" That's an excellent question! In a world with six billion people, how can God use any one person to do anything good? One doesn't seem like a very big number.

Remember the story of Jesus feeding thousands of people with just five loaves and two fish? In John 6 we read that Jesus had been ministering and teaching one day, and thousands of folks were following him everywhere. Jesus knows they're hungry, so he turns to his disciples to see if they have a plan to feed everyone. Jesus asks Philip where they could buy bread for everyone.

Can you imagine being Philip? Jesus was testing Philip because Jesus already had a solution to the problem. Talk about a pop quiz!

The solution wasn't passing the buckets for an offering. No one ran down to the ATM or called Domino's. The answer was in the hands of a boy who'd brought five loaves of bread and a couple of fish. Not much food! Not even enough to feed Jesus' twelve closest disciples. There's no way it could satisfy thousands—that would be impossible, right? Wrong!

> Jesus just needed someone willing to do the possible so he could do the impossible.

Jesus took the bread, said a prayer, and passed food to everyone. Then he grabbed the fish and did the same thing. Not only did everyone eat, but there were twelve baskets of leftover bread (which weren't nearly as smelly as the twelve baskets of leftover fish). Jesus just needed someone willing to do the possible so he could do the impossible.

Who made that miracle happen? It wasn't a big crowd or committee. It wasn't some rich guy rolling in on his chariot with spinners. It was a boy who was willing to offer the little he had (do the possible), so Jesus could do a lot with it (do the impossible).

You might look at your life and see yourself as "just" one person. Maybe you look at your own SHAPE and you can't imagine how God could use it. If so, you're not alone. I know a lot of people who think they're not worthy enough. But, I want to encourage you to review the answers to your SHAPE profile on pages 99-110 and think again about your unique SHAPE. Then, I want you to start serving. I want you to do the possible.

It's true, you are only one person. But your sacrifice, your passion, your personality, your experiences, your talents, your spiritual gifts can be multiplied far beyond your wildest dreams when they're used for the One who isn't trapped by the word *impossible*. You give God the possible (you and your SHAPE) and he does the impossible.

Consider using these simple words from the prophet Isaiah: "Here I am! Send me!" (Check out Isaiah 6 for all the details.) Have a willing heart. Express a humble attitude, be willing to serve, find a friend to encourage you—and you'll never be "just" one person in God's hands.

AGE IS IRRELEVANT

Have you ever heard a pastor or some other adult say, "I believe teenagers are the future of the church"? Every time I hear that statement, it makes me cringe. I understand the heart behind those words, but I don't believe teenagers are the future of the church. I believe they're the church of today. The church of today is you!

You might wonder...what's the difference? Well, if you're the "church of the future," you really don't have much to offer right now. And that's not true. God doesn't place any age restrictions on making a difference in this world. You don't have to wait until you're older to discover, develop, and direct your Kingdom Impact.

David was young when he battled and defeated Goliath. Samuel was young when he heard God's voice in the tabernacle. Mary was young when she gave birth to Jesus. Jeremiah thought he was too young to be used by God, but he wasn't. According to the apostle Paul, Timothy's youth was a benefit, not an obstacle. It's quite possible that some of Jesus' disciples (the ones you read about in the Bible) may have been around your age (or just a little bit older). God doesn't look at someone's birth certificate to determine if they're old enough to have Kingdom Impact. God looks at the heart!

Remember that kid with the five loaves and two fish? Jesus didn't reject his donation just because he wasn't old enough to vote. The disciples were skeptical—of course, these are the same guys who tried to keep children from hanging out with Jesus (see Mark 10). But Jesus wanted to spend time with the children and even went so far as to use children as the example of what we all must do to get into heaven (have a childlike faith).

I've learned young people are willing to dream big dreams. You believe God is able to do incredible things in and through you. That's why you're the church of today. The church needs *your* Kingdom Impact *now!*

Age isn't an issue for Zach Hunter, a 15-year-old from Georgia who's become deeply involved in rescuing modern-day slaves. Zach learned a few years ago that many people are still forced to live as slaves today. Zach didn't think, "You know, when I grow up, I should do something about that." He decided to make a difference now—and he's never let his age be an obstacle.

At first, some people didn't take him seriously. But within the last couple of years, Zach has gained a national platform to tell people about the reality of slavery in the 21st century. He's been on TV and radio. He's been interviewed by the biggest newspapers and magazines in the country. He has even written a book titled, *Be the Change*. He's just one guy. He's one *young* guy making a difference for a cause he believes in and for the God he follows.

I've spent a little bit of time with Zach. He's not a superhero. He's a very normal teenager who isn't afraid of being used by God. He has been willing to do the possible and allow God to do the impossible.

You're not the church of tomorrow. You're the church of today.

> You're not the church of tomorrow. You're the church of today.

CONTINUE TO DREAM

What do you want God to do with your life? This isn't a selfish question. It's a dreamer question. How would you like God to use you for his glory? How do you see your SHAPE unfolding and affecting your Kingdom Impact? Keep dreaming. Even though you're finishing this book and you have answers to the SHAPE questions...keep dreaming.

As I mentioned earlier, it's okay to have big dreams if your goal is to honor God, not yourself. God wants you to dream big.

Dream of working as a missionary in another country.

Dream of becoming a teacher and investing your life in the next generation.

Dream of starting a chain of businesses that will provide jobs to inner-city families.

Dream of using technology to battle disease in developing nations.

Dream of writing books that will inspire, encourage, and motivate other people to grow closer to God.

Dream of producing music that will impact lives because of its creativity and positive message.

Revive old dreams. Fuel current dreams. Dream new dreams. Pursue future dreams. Dream today about how God can use your Kingdom Impact for his honor.

PRAY FOR ETERNAL RESULTS

Ultimately, your Kingdom Impact needs God's blessing. You can dream and plan and work, but you also need to pray. Sometimes it's easy to believe that if you want good results, all you have to do is work hard. That's not always true. Hard work is important, but the results aren't up to you. The results are in God's hands.

That reminds me of something Paul wrote in a letter to the Christians in Corinth. Paul had done a ton of work among the people in Corinth. But he reminded them that neither he nor another church leader, Apollos, could take credit for the changes in their lives. "I planted the seed, Apollos watered it, but God has been making it grow" (1 Corinthians 3:6).

Your hard work alone won't produce eternal change in anyone's life. It's important that you *do* work hard, and you need to be faithful in using the gifts and abilities God's given you. But remember it is God who produces change in you, in me, and in others.

LET YOUR KINGDOM IMPACT BEGIN

Are you ready? We've been talking for a long time. You've been asking great questions. The barista has refilled our drinks several times. Our Starbucks conversation is about to end. It's time for you to prepare to take action.

These ideas aren't worth much if you don't apply them to your life. I could tell you many more stories about people from the Bible and teenagers I know who have discovered, developed, and directed their SHAPE for a Kingdom Impact. But it's up to you to respond to the challenge. Are you ready?

> These ideas aren't worth much if you don't apply them to your life.

You're a masterpiece created by the Master Artist. He doesn't make mistakes. He loves you and has huge dreams for your life. Now you have the opportunity to continue what God has started. I'm praying that God will strengthen you and show you just how special you are. Live a life that honors God. Use your spiritual gifts, your passions, your abilities, your personality, and your experiences to change your world for God's glory.

I'll be cheering you on with great excitement, as you run with God in the next leg of your race. Actually, I'd love to hear all about what you've learned and how you are seeking to use your unique SHAPE to make a difference in this world. Please go to www.dougfields.com or email erik@shapediscovery.com and share your story with me. Remember: You're gifted! Congratulations!

FOR REFLECTION, JOURNALING, OR SMALL-GROUP DISCUSSION

What did you learn from this chapter about how you can make a difference today?

What opportunities has God given you to help change your world today?

Who can help you be strong and courageous as you take your next steps?

What dream are you trusting God to turn into reality? Are you praying for eternal results from that dream?

SHAPE

APPENDIXES

APPENDIX A

SPIRITUAL GIFTS DESCRIPTIONS

Here's a list that offers some explanation about each of the spiritual
gifts discussed in chapter 2. After
you read each definition, think
about the experiences you've had
while serving others and then circle
"yes" if you feel you probably have
this gift, "maybe" if you might have
this gift, or "no" if you think there's
little chance God has given you this
spiritual gift. When you finish, transfer
your answers to your SHAPE profile on
page 101. I want to reemphasize here
what I wrote in chapter 2—these are
only human-made questions. Answering a few questions won't tell you what
your spiritual gift is—but this exercise

may give you a direction to begin the journey of discovering it.

Administration: Organizing and helping others become more efficient in reaching their ministry goals. People with this spiritual gift...

- Effectively organize people to reach their ministry goals.

- Usually have specific plans to reach clearly defined goals.

- Get other people involved, making it possible to accomplish more.

- Enjoy making decisions.

- Understand what needs to be done for dreams to become a reality.

I think I may have this gift (circle one): Yes   Maybe   No

Apostleship: Launching and leading new ministries that advance God's purposes and expand his kingdom. The original Greek meaning of the word *apostle* is "sent one" (literally, one sent with authority, or as an ambassador). People with this spiritual gift...

- Are eager to start new ministries for God.

- Often welcome risky new challenges.

- Enjoy making a difference in the lives of both believers and unbelievers.

- Want to be known as representatives of Jesus in their culture.

- Willingly work hard to see ministries reach their full potential for God.

I think I may have this gift (circle one): Yes Maybe No

Discernment: Recognizing truth or error within a message, person, or event. People with this spiritual gift...

- Find it easy to "read" others, and are often right.

- Recognize the spiritual source of a message—whether it is from God, from Satan, or human.

- Recognize inconsistencies in others.

- Easily identify people's true motives and agendas.

- Know when the truth is twisted or communicated with error.

I think I may have this gift (circle one): Yes Maybe No

Encouragement: Helping others live God-centered lives through inspiration, encouragement, counseling, and motivation. People with this spiritual gift...

- Want to inspire others to become more like Jesus.

- Rejoice with people who have overcome tough times with God's help.

- Seek opportunities to help others reach their full potential as followers of Jesus.

- Find ways to encourage through words or actions.

- Celebrate when friends succeed.

I think I may have this gift (circle one): Yes   Maybe   No

Evangelism: Sharing the love of Jesus with others in a way that draws them toward a personal relationship with God. People with this spiritual gift...

- Look for ways to build friendships with nonbelievers.

- Sense when a person is open to the message of good news.

- Have likely seen friends come to faith in Jesus.

- Help bring others to Christ through acts of love.

- Deeply care for friends and strangers who don't know Jesus.

I think I may have this gift (circle one): Yes   Maybe   No

Faith: Stepping out in faith to see God's purposes accomplished, trusting him to handle obstacles along the way. People with this spiritual gift...

- Welcome risk for God.
- Enjoy unpredictable situations.
- Are challenged by ideas others say are impossible.
- Often have a passionate prayer life.
- Have great God-confidence in their efforts.

I think I may have this gift (circle one): Yes Maybe No

Giving: Joyfully supporting and funding various God-honoring efforts through financial contributions beyond the tithe. People with this spiritual gift...

- Plan and purposely give more than the tithe (10 percent) to see God's kingdom advanced.
- Generally prefer their donations remain anonymous or low-profile.
- Strategically seek ways to increase their resources so they can give more for God's use.
- See their resources as tools for God's use.
- Recognize God's ultimate ownership of everything (including their money).

I think I may have this gift (circle one): Yes Maybe No

Healing: Restoring to health or healing, beyond traditional and natural means, those who are sick, hurting, and suffering. People with this spiritual gift...

- Believe firmly that people can be super-naturally healed.
- Pray specifically to be used by God to heal others.
- Fully realize that healing occurs only by God's permission.
- View medicine as a means God may choose for healing.
- Embrace their gift as from the hand of God, and as a specific way to bring Him glory.

I think I may have this gift (circle one): Yes Maybe No

Helping: Offering others assistance. This is sometimes referred to as the spiritual gift of "helps" or "service." People with this spiritual gift...

- Enjoy and seek ways to serve behind the scenes.
- Look for ways to help friends succeed.
- Are often focused on details.
- Look for ways to assist others in need.
- Do not seek recognition for their efforts.

I think I may have this gift (circle one): Yes Maybe No

Hospitality: Providing others with a warm and welcoming environment and meeting some of their basic needs. People with this spiritual gift...

- Make other people feel valued and cared for.
- Look for peers who may go unnoticed in a crowd.
- Want people to feel loved and welcomed.
- View their home as God's property, given to them expressly to make others feel welcome.
- Promote deep friendships wherever they are.

I think I may have this gift (circle one): Yes Maybe No

Interpretation: Understanding, at a specific time, God's message when spoken by another person who is using a special language (tongues) unknown to the others in attendance. People with this spiritual gift tend to...

- Have a clear idea of what God is saying, even though the language used by the speaker is unknown to them at the specific time.
- Be able to translate words and messages of God in a way that builds up, comforts, and challenges believers.

- Communicate the meaning of sounds, words, and utterances that glorify God, made by others.

I think I may have this gift (circle one): Yes Maybe No

Knowledge: Communicating God's truth to others in a way that promotes justice, honesty, and understanding. People with this spiritual gift...

- Devote lots of time to reading and studying the Bible.

- Love to share biblical insight.

- Enjoy helping others understand the Bible better.

- Benefit from time invested studying and researching Scripture.

- Take delight in answering tough questions about God's Word.

I think I may have this gift (circle one): Yes Maybe No

Leadership: Casting vision, stimulating spiritual growth, applying strategies, and leading others to achieve results. People with this spiritual gift...

- Usually have "big ideas" for God and the ability to rally other people to accomplish those ideas.

- Are naturally drawn toward leadership roles.

- Find it easy to motivate people—both individually and in teams—to work together in achieving goals for God.
- Naturally grasp the "big picture."
- Willingly give responsibilities and tasks to other people.

I think I may have this gift (circle one): Yes Maybe No

Mercy: Ministering to those who suffer physically, emotionally, spiritually, or relationally. Their actions are characterized by love, care, compassion, and kindness toward others. People with this spiritual gift...

- Gravitate toward opportunities to practically help others in need.
- Devote significant time in prayer for those who are hurting.
- Tend to place the needs of others ahead of their own.
- Genuinely feel other people's pain and suffering.
- Find fulfillment when visiting people in need—in hospitals, nursing homes, prisons, orphanages, villages, or wherever God directs them.

I think I may have this gift (circle one): Yes Maybe No

Miracles: Being used through supernatural acts that point to God and his power. People with this spiritual gift...

- Recognize prayer as a supernatural vehicle through which God acts in the lives of people on earth.
- Give credit and thanks to God alone for supernatural works.
- Realize miracles only occur when God wills them to happen.
- See themselves as instruments for God's use.
- Pray and look for supernatural results whenever they encounter impossible life situations.

I think I may have this gift (circle one): Yes   Maybe   No

Pastoring: Taking spiritual responsibility for a group of believers and helping them live lives directed by God's Word. "Shepherding" is another word used for this gift. People with this spiritual gift...

- Want to help others reach their full potential as followers of Christ.
- Enjoy serving others and look for opportunities to do this.
- Are good at developing personal, trust-based relationships with a small group of people.

- Are drawn toward meeting the needs of others, willingly giving time to help them with spiritual issues.

- Believe that people are more important than projects.

I think I may have this gift (circle one): Yes   Maybe   No

Prophecy: Offering messages from God that comfort, encourage, guide, warn, or reveal sin in a way that leads to one's repentance and spiritual growth. The original Greek meaning of this word is "to speak forth the truth." The gift of prophecy includes both "forth telling" (preaching), and "foretelling" (revelation). People with this spiritual gift...

- Are known for publicly communicating God's Word, using a variety of means.

- Love to share strong biblical ideas with others.

- View themselves as God's tool, ready to be used by the Holy Spirit in changing lives.

- Find it easy to confront others' motives when they are not up to God's standards.

- Frequently receive and share messages directly from God for comforting, challenging, and confronting his people.

I think I may have this gift (circle one): Yes   Maybe   No

Teaching: Presenting good Bible teaching in relevant ways, helping people gain a strong and mature spiritual education. People with this spiritual gift...

- Study Scripture intensely so they can help others apply its principles and truth.

- Enjoy making the Bible clear and understandable to friends.

- See how biblical principles remain relevant to today's culture.

- Are good at helping others learn to study the Bible.

- Recognize a variety of ways to effectively communicate the Word of God, including speaking.

I think I may have this gift (circle one): Yes   Maybe   No

Tongues: Communicating God's message in a special language unknown to the speaker. People with this spiritual gift tend to...

- Believe God is prompting them to communicate his message, often through prayer, in a specific language unknown to them.

- Intercede for others in prayer using unknown words, sounds, and utterances.

- Desire opportunities to pray, using these unknown languages for God's glory.

- Share with others words and/or messages of God given to them using unknown languages.

- Comfort or exhort others using unknown languages inspired by God.

I think I may have this gift (circle one): Yes   Maybe   No

Wisdom: Making wise decisions and counseling others with solid advice, all in accordance with God's will. People with this spiritual gift...

- Enjoy speaking biblical insights into life situations.

- Have friends who come to them for advice or wisdom.

- Enjoy counseling others.

- Are known for making correct decisions and judgments.

- Recognize God as the primary source of wisdom and direction.

I think I may have this gift (circle one): Yes   Maybe   No

Now look over your answers and choose five gifts you feel you may have. Then you can record them on page 101 of your SHAPE profile. (Start with the ones where you answered "yes." Add the "maybes" if space permits.)

ABILITIES

This list includes a bunch of skills that are fairly common, even though some may seem a little "adult" for this kind of book. Be thinking about how God has gifted you today as a teenager, but also be wise enough to know that in a few years you'll be living with adult-type responsibilities. Again, this list isn't complete so please add to it as you think of other abilities that aren't listed. Remember, from God's point of view, no abilities are superior or inferior. All abilities matter to God. Have fun and ask God to awaken you to what you're naturally good at.

Circle the natural abilities you excel at and "love" doing.

1. **Adapting**: The ability to adjust, change, alter, modify.

2. **Analyzing**: The ability to examine, investigate, probe, evaluate.

3. **Building**: The ability to construct, make, assemble.

4. **Coaching**: The ability to prepare, instruct, train, equip, develop.

5. **Communicating**: The ability to share, convey, impart.

6. **Competing**: The ability to contend, win, battle.

7. **Computing**: The ability to add, estimate, total, calculate.

8. **Connecting**: The ability to link together, involve, relate.

9. **Consulting**: The ability to advise, discuss, confer.

10. **Cooking**: The ability to prepare, serve, feed, cater.

11. **Coordinating**: The ability to organize, match, harmonize.

12. **Counseling**: The ability to guide, advise, support, listen, care for.

13. **Creating:** The ability to envision, design, develop.

14. **Decorating**: The ability to beautify, enhance, adorn.

15. **Designing**: The ability to draw, create, picture, outline.

16. **Developing**: The ability to expand, grow, advance, increase.

17. **Directing**: The ability to aim, oversee, manage, supervise.

18. **Editing**: The ability to correct, amend, alter, improve.

19. **Encouraging**: The ability to cheer, inspire, support.

20. **Engineering**: The ability to construct, design, plan.

21. **Facilitating**: The ability to help, aid, assist, make possible.

22. **Forecasting**: The ability to predict, calculate, see trends, patterns, and themes.

23. **Implementing**: The ability to apply, execute, make happen.

24. **Improving**: The ability to better, enhance, further, enrich.

25. **Influencing**: The ability to affect, sway, shape, change.

26. **Landscaping**: The ability to garden, plant, improve.

27. **Leading**: The ability to pave the way, direct, excel, win.

28. **Learning**: The ability to study, gather, understand, improve, expand self.

29. **Managing**: The ability to run, handle, oversee.

30. **Mentoring**: The ability to advise, guide, teach.

31. **Motivating**: The ability to provoke, induce, prompt.

32. **Negotiating**: The ability to discuss, consult, settle.

33. **Operating**: The ability to run mechanical or technical things.

34. **Organizing**: The ability to simplify, arrange, fix, classify, coordinate.

35. **Performing**: The ability to sing, speak, dance, play an instrument, act.

36. **Pioneering**: The ability to bring about something new, groundbreaking, original.

37. **Planning**: The ability to arrange, map out, prepare.

38. **Promoting**: The ability to sell, sponsor, endorse, showcase.

39. **Recruiting**: The ability to draft, enlist, hire, engage.

40. **Repairing**: The ability to fix, mend, restore, heal.

41. **Researching**: The ability to seek, gather, examine, study.

42. **Resourcing**: The ability to furnish, provide, deliver.

43. **Serving**: The ability to help, assist, fulfill.

44. **Strategizing**: The ability to think ahead, calculate, scheme.

45. **Teaching**: The ability to explain, demonstrate, tutor.

46. **Translating**: The ability to interpret, decode, explain, speak.

47. **Traveling**: The ability to journey, visit, explore.

48. **Visualizing**: The ability to picture, imagine, envision, dream, conceptualize.

49. **Welcoming**: The ability to entertain, greet, embrace, make comfortable.

50. **Writing**: The ability to compose, create, record.

If you circled more than five of the 50 items, go back and pick the five that most define you. Then turn to page 103, and record five abilities that most reflect who you are.

SHAPE
A SPECIAL NOTE FOR YOUTH WORKERS

A FEW TIPS TO MAKE THIS SHAPE IDEA WORK WITHIN YOUR MINISTRY

The best youth workers I know are the ones constantly hunting for great ideas to strengthen both their ministries and their students. If you're reading this page, you are probably that kind of youth worker. If so, I believe this book can be a valuable tool to help you take your teenagers to a deeper level in their faith commitment and their ministry development.

Whether you have all your students read this book and discuss it in small groups or just give it to a particular student and meet one-on-one, I want to thank you for encouraging teenagers to realize they're gifted and they have something to offer the kingdom. As one youth worker to the next, I applaud you for caring so deeply about the students God has entrusted to your care. Thank you for investing your time and energy into teenagers' lives! Helping them discover their God-given SHAPE will require some effort from you, but the return on your relational and spiritual investment will be incredible.

Below you'll find several tips that may help you maximize your investments with the teenagers who are reading this book. By following these suggestions, you'll strengthen what your students are learning about how gifted they are.

1. ACCEPT YOUR RESPONSIBILITY

I like to say, "Spot it, you got it." That means if students in your ministry come to you for help (as the book suggests they should), please view it as a privilege to help guide them. The apostle Paul talks about "encouraging, comforting and urging [others] to live lives worthy of God" (1 Thessalonians 2:12). As a youth worker you fully understand that one of your roles is to nurture teenagers in their relationship with God. Rejoice that you have the privilege to help guide a teenager to discover his or her unique SHAPE and put that discovery into practice. I have taken hundreds of teenagers through this SHAPE process over the last 25+ years, and I've found great joy in helping them put into practice what's in this book. I love telling them, "Congratulations...You're Gifted!"—and so will you!

2. ENCOURAGE THEIR EFFORT

When students ask for your help, please let them know you are proud of them for seeking help. Even if you can't meet with them for a few days, let them know that you're excited about their journey and the discovery of their SHAPE. Your encouragement will help them stay motivated. It's amazing what a little encouragement will do for a teenager.

3. SHARE SOME OF YOUR PERSONAL SHAPE DISCOVERY

When you talk with teenagers, be sure to share some of your own personal SHAPE-discovery experiences. Let them know where you struggled, were confused, found answers, paused and thought, prayed, etc....In order to do this with authenticity, I would encourage you to read through the book yourself and answer the SHAPE profile questions on pages 101-110. I think you'll find it to be an easy read, and you may want to ask all your youth ministry leaders to read through the book so they can better accompany teenagers through the process.

4. LISTEN MORE THAN YOU TALK

Although I do want you to share some of your experiences when meeting with young people, I really want you to listen to them more than you talk about yourself. Be in prayer and ask for God's wisdom to give you specific and insightful questions that will help them reach a little deeper than, "I don't know." Ask them to share what they've learned from each chapter and how they believe God has made them special. Become a master at asking the types of questions that prompt them to think and guide them to want to use their uniqueness for God's glory.

5. AFFIRM THEIR UNIQUENESS

I'd love to assume this happens naturally, but I've watched too many caring adults be more concerned with answers than with the journey. Helping teenagers discover their SHAPE is more than having them regurgitate correct answers to the SHAPE profile questions. Throughout your conversation, encourage their answers, affirm their learnings, and cheer them on since they may be insecure in some of their self-discovery. They may not be getting much affirmation at home or from their friends, so cheer loudly for them as you guide them.

6. GET THEM INTO A MINISTRY OPPORTUNITY SOON

When they reach chapter 7, readers will be challenged to go after their Kingdom Impact based on their SHAPE. It's important they not pause too long at this point. Help them find opportunities for ministry ASAP...even if the ministry is not the perfect fit for a particular student's unique SHAPE. If they have spent the time reading this book and answering questions, they'll be ready to do something. Get them serving and build on their enthusiasm and momentum. If you're not sure where to use them, begin with a need you currently have in your ministry. Your need + their SHAPE = a ministry opportunity.

> Your need + their SHAPE = a ministry opportunity.

7. REVIEW THEIR PROGRESS

This is where your investment *really* begins. Yes, you have put in a lot of time, prayer, and energy up to this point, but only time will reveal if a young person is serving in an area that best expresses his or her personal SHAPE. When students make the commitment to go through the process of filling out the SHAPE profile, we must make a commitment to meet with them occasionally to review, debrief, and make any necessary course corrections.

If the content of this book feels like it may be too much for all the students in your ministry, begin with the more mature, ministry-minded teenagers. Going through this process with even one student can be unbelievably rewarding. I ask my youth ministry volunteers to (a) read and understand the material, (b) find one teenager per month to read the book, and (c) meet with them to help them get into a ministry based on their SHAPE. You'll be amazed at what can happen to a youth ministry when one teenager begins serving based on his or her SHAPE... incredible things will happen!